AF866005

# THE PRICE OF BEING RIGHT

***Why Defending an Error Costs More Than Making One***

Second Edition

**Alexander Chanthunya, LL.M (AU)**

Copyright © 2026 Alexander Chanthunya, LL.M (AU)

All rights reserved.

No part of this book may be reproduced, stored in a retrieval system, or transmitted in any form or by any means, electronic, mechanical, photocopying, recording, or otherwise, without the prior written permission of the copyright holder, except in the case of brief quotations embodied in critical reviews and certain other noncommercial uses permitted by copyright law.

This book is a work of nonfiction. It reflects the author's personal experience, judgment, and recollection, offered in good faith. The events described are presented as accurately as available records and memory permit; where the author's records were incomplete, the text says so directly rather than reconstructing detail from imagination.

Second Edition
ISBN: 979-8-9970327-8-4

# Contents

INTRODUCTION

# What This Book Is About

You make a judgment before breakfast and may not call it one. You decide that the pain in your shoulder can wait. A message can go unanswered for another day. You decide that a person who disappointed you once has explained themselves well enough, or that the next explanation can be heard tomorrow, and by midday you have made dozens more. Most disappear because most do not demand an account. A missed turn is corrected at the next light, and a poor choice of restaurant becomes a story. A bad purchase goes into a cupboard. Life contains a great deal of mercy for the small errors that pass through it.

Expensive judgments often begin in the same ordinary way. Something no longer fits the facts. You notice it, perhaps only as a pressure in the background, then give it a name that makes postponement sound sensible. You are waiting for more information. You do not want to overreact. Perhaps you have already invested too much to leave casually. You want to be fair, and each sentence may be reasonable on its own.

Together they can keep you from reopening a decision after the decision has begun to fail. That is a familiar human problem, not a rare defect of character.

It is easy to picture the expensive error as a wild choice made in a burst of confidence. You move too fast, ignore every warning, then suffer the obvious result. Sometimes, in ordinary life, that is exactly what happens. More often, the error becomes costly because it survives the moment when it should have been examined. You may have made the first decision for sound reasons. Your mistake comes later, when the reasons weaken and you keep treating their earlier strength as proof of their present force. Being wrong is not itself the expense. Every adult is wrong, often and quietly. Defending the wrongness after it has become visible creates the expense.

A bad conversation has a familiar course, even when nobody has named it. In the first hours, a person can still recall the word that stung, the look on the other person's face, the point they meant to make. Soon memory begins arranging the episode into a case against the other party, and the injured person rehearses the part where they were misunderstood. A friend hears enough of the story for the speaker's conduct to seem inevitable. By the time the relationship grows colder, the original subject may be almost beside the point, and what keeps the disagreement alive is the difficulty of admitting that the first account was incomplete. More than the argument is now being protected. The person who made it is being protected as well.

The same thing happens in decisions that appear more practical. Suppose a driver hears a faint sound in the car when turning left. Nothing about the sound seems dramatic at first. The vehicle still starts. It still gets the driver where they need to go. The radio is turned down once for a listen, then back up because the sound has not become a clear diagnosis. A week later it seems probably nothing, partly because the car has been driven all week without disaster, and the sound returns at a junction. Booking an inspection can seem excessive when nobody even knows what is wrong. A person who is cautious with money can think this in complete sincerity. Perhaps the car is fine for now, as it may be. No noise necessarily predicts a major repair. Yet the question has changed without being acknowledged. It began as a question about whether there was a noise. Now it is a question about whether the noise has yet forced action. The absence of catastrophe has become evidence that no inspection is due. If a mechanic later identifies a small fault that has become a larger one, the costly part will not be hearing the first sound. It will be the private series of decisions that turned each further sound into a reason to wait.

Nothing about that person is foolish. You may be that person next week. You have responsibilities, competing bills and a reasonable suspicion that people sometimes waste money by treating every uncertainty as an emergency. The ability to tolerate uncertainty is useful. A person who cannot do so will spend every day running after reassurances. Even useful tolerance must eventually have a boundary. At some point, patience stops being a response to incomplete evidence and becomes a way of avoiding evidence that has become inconvenient, and that boundary is hard to see from inside a choice because the mind that drew it has an interest in keeping it where it is.

Few of us have a reliable system for noticing the change. We may notice an outcome, especially when it produces a bill or an argument or a lost opportunity. We are less likely to examine the succession of judgments that let the outcome grow. The story we tell afterwards is usually too simple. We say that we trusted the wrong person, chose the wrong course, missed a warning or had bad luck. Every one of these explanations may contain some truth. None tells us whether we had a point at which we could have reconsidered, or why we did not use it.

The same structure appears in a renovation when a person receives an estimate for a repair that has to be done. The necessary work then begins in earnest. A concealed problem appears behind a wall, then another, and each addition sounds plausible because older houses contain hidden things and work cannot stop forever every time a surprise appears. Before very long, the estimate rises again. A contractor may offer a coherent explanation, and an owner may not want to accuse anyone of bad faith without proof. Stopping midway would also leave the home partly opened and the earlier spending apparently wasted. The next amount is approved while the owner tells themselves that the original plan is still mostly intact.

At some later point, perhaps when the total is far above the figure that first seemed manageable, the owner may be unable to say what decision is now being made. Is the work being finished, the earlier spending being saved, the contractor being trusted, the inconvenience of a dispute being avoided, or are all these motives present at once? Accepting the first estimate was not the difficulty. Each revision was treated as a continuation of the first decision when it should have required a new one. The old approval had acquired authority it did not deserve.

Consider a course of study that no longer seems to lead anywhere its student wants to go. The student began because the subject was interesting, because a teacher saw promise, or because the programme had a clear next step. Two years later, the work may have changed. Perhaps the field feels narrower than expected, and the student is doing well enough that leaving appears wasteful, yet not well enough to feel committed. Family members begin asking serious questions about graduation. Friends describe the job prospects in confident terms, and the student answers with the same words already used before. Each completed term becomes an argument for another term. The investment can seem impossible to abandon. There is truth there: time matters, money matters and credentials can matter. Still, sunk time cannot choose. It can only make a new choice feel disloyal to an old one.

An honest question is not whether the years already spent have value. Those earlier years do have real value. It is whether the next year has value on its own terms. That question can feel almost rude because it removes the protection of the past. The future cannot be governed solely by the need to vindicate an earlier self.

This book concerns the point at which a judgment ought to be reopened, and why people can pass it without stopping when the earlier decision has already acquired the comfort and authority of a settled thing and no longer feels open to inspection. Stock trading makes that process unusually visible. Its subject is not the market in the ordinary sense. It is not a guide to picking shares. It is not an argument that a reader should trade, or a warning that readers should never trade. Here, the market supplies a severe little laboratory in which habits that remain hidden elsewhere acquire a number, a clock and a consequence.

In daily life, a person can make a poor decision and never know whether it was poor. They may move house, change jobs, decline an invitation, trust a new partner, keep an old subscription, delay a medical appointment or enter a disagreement from which nobody emerges wiser. Years may then pass without a clear answer. Any outcome contains too many variables to isolate one person's part in it, and a favourable result can receive too much credit while a bad one receives too much blame assigned to luck. Often both accounts are used at different moments. Judgment has been tested, but not in a way that lets its test be seen clearly.

Trading strips away some of that delay, and a share is a small unit of ownership in a company. When someone buys it, they are making a judgment that it is worth buying at that price for a reason of their own. Prices change in public, and the person can see, almost at once, what the market is offering for the same share. If the position is closed, meaning the share is sold after it has been bought, the result becomes a number. Money has either arrived or left, and the price does not explain everything, but it does not allow a person to pretend that nothing has happened.

That does not mean the market offers a moral verdict, and a trade can lose money even if the reasoning was sound, just as another can make money for reasons that have nothing to do with skill and never deserve the name of judgment. Price is not wisdom. It is simply hard to ignore. It turns a private opinion into something that can be measured in minutes, hours or days. A person who says, "I think this is a good idea," is brought quickly to a more demanding question: what will you do if the evidence does not agree with you?

That is why the setting matters, and trading places your judgment in an environment where every decision receives a price and where the price keeps moving whether you inspect it or not. It removes many of the ordinary protections that make self-deception comfortable. You cannot say the market failed to respond. You cannot attribute the result to a vague atmosphere in the office or to a relative's temperament. You can find plenty of explanations, of course. Markets offer no shortage of explanations. Yet the number remains in view. It may go down while you continue to believe that waiting will make the problem disappear. Now the judgment is no longer hidden inside a larger life. It sits in front of you with a changing value.

This is judgment under a microscope, and the microscope does not make the specimen more important than the person looking at it. It makes its structure easier to see. A reader who never intends to buy a share may recognise the same movements in a stalled conversation, a project that has passed its budget or a promise that has ceased to be mutual, and the scale differs in outward form. Its underlying sequence does not differ at all. You form a view. You commit something to it. Then fresh facts arrive at the door. You decide whether those facts modify the view or become material for defending it.

Trading language may be unfamiliar, so it is worth making the scene plain before asking anything of it, and to trade intraday is to buy and sell during the same market day. Scalping is an especially fast version of this practice: a person tries to make small gains from brief movements in price, then repeats the process. Such a holding period may be short enough that reflection becomes part of the problem, and a price moves. The live screen changes again before you decide. A person decides, and the next opportunity appears before the meaning of the first decision has settled.

A position is what a trader currently owns or owes in a particular share. If shares of a company were bought this morning, that position remains until they are sold. A position can show a gain or a loss while it remains open. That changing figure is called an unrealised gain or unrealised loss, and "unrealised" can sound harmless, as if the loss were only an idea. Yet the loss is not merely an idea. If a trader paid one hundred dollars for something now worth eighty, the twenty-dollar loss has happened in the only sense that matters to available money. The sale has not been completed, but the price tells the trader what could be obtained now. Leaving the position open does not erase the loss. It postpones the moment at which the trader agrees to call it one. The loss has already occurred in substance. Your agreement with that fact has not.

That distinction is central beyond trading, and a loss can be real before it is acknowledged. A business can continue after its customers have gone elsewhere. A friendship can continue after trust has worn away, and a house can hold its outward shape while a leak worsens inside a wall. Someone may postpone the act that makes the loss final because finality feels like failure. In the meantime, the cost continues, and some losses recover. Others remain losses despite every delay. The point is neither to surrender quickly nor to treat every adverse fact as final. It is to notice when language has begun disguising a present condition as a future possibility.

A stop-loss is a standing instruction to exit a position if the price reaches a defined point. It is a modest device with an ambitious idea behind it. Before pressure arrives, the person specifies a condition under which the earlier judgment will no longer govern. Such an instruction does not prove that the chosen point is wise, and no number can remove uncertainty. It does make a fact harder to bargain with after the fact has appeared. By setting a stop, the person gives the future self less room to rewrite the terms in a favourable direction.

You do similar things outside the market, though often less formally. You tell yourself that if a contractor cannot produce a revised written estimate, the work pauses. You decide that if a doctor's office does not return a call by a certain date, you will seek another appointment. With a sibling, you may agree that a conversation will end if voices rise, and such rules may be revised in a real emergency, because life is not an automatic machine. Their purpose is not to impose rigidity. Their purpose is to preserve a decision made before fear, pride, urgency or hope has taken control of the room.

A watchlist is simply a list of shares a trader intends to keep an eye on, and a ticker is the short label used to identify a share on a screen. Volume is the number of shares changing hands during a period. Volatility describes how sharply or quickly a price is moving, and the spread is the small gap between the price a buyer is currently offering and the price a seller is currently asking. Each word names part of a crowded environment. None tells a person what judgment to make. They describe the field. They do not supply the discipline required to move within it.

These tools belong in that same category. They were good tools. That needs to be said without qualification because a weak instrument would make the wrong story too easy, allowing every later error to be placed on equipment that had not in fact failed. If the screens were toys, or the services were careless, then the lesson could be reduced to a bad purchase. It cannot. The equipment was well regarded, capable and used by people who take market information seriously. It performed the functions for which it was built.

Its limits were honest from the beginning. Its uses were fully real. Finviz is a stock screener, and a screener is a way of filtering thousands of listed companies until a trader sees only those that match conditions he has selected. One might ask it to show shares within a certain price range, shares with unusually heavy trading volume or shares moving more than usual. Its usefulness lies in speed and breadth, and Finviz also offers a heat map, which lets a person see large portions of the market at a glance through a field of changing colour. It is a sensible response to an obvious problem: no one can inspect every listed company by hand.

Trade Ideas is a real-time scanner, and a scanner differs from a screener in the same way a live alarm differs from a prepared search. A screener answers a question you set in advance. The scanner watches continuously and alerts you when conditions appear, and Trade Ideas is respected for pattern recognition and for bringing activity to a trader's attention more quickly than a person could find it by manually watching many shares at once. In a fast market, that capacity is real. It may be exactly what a trader wants, and the scanner sees movement. It cannot decide what the movement should mean to the particular person watching it.

TradingView is charting, and a chart turns changing prices into a picture over time. You do not need market experience to understand its appeal. A line can show in seconds whether something has risen, fallen, paused or swung violently, and TradingView is widely regarded as an exceptional charting interface. It has a large community of users who publish their own analyses, which is why many people encounter it before they know much else about markets. It gives a trader a clear visual account of what prices have done. It does not say whether the viewer is seeing evidence or seeing what he hopes to find.

Thinkorswim is an execution platform from a major brokerage, and execution sounds grander than it is. It means the part of the system through which a person actually enters an order to buy or sell. Thinkorswim offers professional-grade order entry, options analysis and paper trading, and paper trading lets someone practise with simulated transactions instead of real money. Such features allow a person to test how a method might work, but a simulation cannot reproduce the full pressure of a real loss. A platform can make action precise. It cannot determine whether action is called for.

An advantage can become a shelter when it supplies the appearance of care without the practice of reconsideration. You have probably met this form of avoidance in a setting far from finance. A manager spends weeks refining a presentation because each revision is useful, then never addresses the disagreement that is blocking the team. A couple researches every detail of a move, compares districts and builds elaborate spreadsheets, then avoids the basic question of whether both people want the same life. Someone else reads reviews until the purchase feels justified, then treats the volume of research as a reason not to admit that they do not need the thing at all. Work has occurred. Information has been gathered, and the missing decision has merely been protected by the activity around it.

The monthly costs make the point in financial form, and Finviz cost $39.50 a month. Trade Ideas cost $254 a month. Together they cost $293.50 a month, or roughly $4,990 across those seventeen months, and that arithmetic is not presented as a grievance against either service. They delivered access to the sort of information they advertised. Paying for them was not evidence of recklessness. It was evidence of a belief that better sight would improve judgment. In many contexts, you would share that belief. You should. The mistake begins when better sight is treated as a replacement for the willingness to see an unwelcome conclusion.

The author had reason to expect more from his own habits of judgment. He qualified as a lawyer in 1978 and practised until he ceased in 2016. He is now a licensed Maryland realtor and mortgage broker. Over seventeen months, he lost more than $20,000 through intraday scalping of various stocks, and those are spare facts. They do not establish a diagnosis. They do establish the question that gives this account its force: how could forty-seven years of trained judgment fail to travel into a setting that made judgment so immediate?

Professional training has genuine value. It teaches habits of attention. It can require a person to distinguish what is known from what is assumed, to document a conclusion, to hear the case against his first view and to recognise that confident speech is not evidence. Such habits improve work. They may also depend more on their setting than the person who has acquired them wants to believe. When a client can ask for an explanation, when a file records the sequence, when another professional can challenge an assumption or when a rule requires disclosure, good habits have external support. They are not simply private virtues carried intact from one room to another.

You may have your own version of that discovery. You are patient with other people's problems, then impatient with your own. You follow a process at work, then abandon it when a personal decision feels urgent. At work, you can ask a colleague the exact question that would expose a weak plan, then fail to ask it of yourself because nobody else is waiting for the answer, and competence is often local. It grows in conditions that reward it and can lose force when those conditions disappear. A person may carry the language of a discipline into a new setting without carrying the structure that made the language meaningful.

A trader's position makes this recruitment unusually plain. Suppose a trader buys a share because a particular movement seems to signal further demand. Price falls. The trader may decide that the fall is temporary, and that can be a rational judgment. Then price falls further. The trader may decide the market has misunderstood the same signal, and that too may be possible. At some point the story may change from an account of the share to an account of the trader. The question is no longer what the price means. It has become a question about what can be said to avoid closing the position. In language, the difference is slight. It is large in consequence.

No trading experience is needed to recognise that turn. It appears when a person keeps a subscription because cancelling would mean admitting it is never used. The same movement appears when someone continues to attend a committee that no longer serves its purpose because leaving would look disloyal. It appears again in the defence of a purchase long after its owner has stopped enjoying it, or in the pursuit of a job that has become intolerable because it was described too proudly to too many people. The original choice may have been good. There may still be reasons to continue. The question is whether those reasons are still being evaluated, or whether the honour of the earlier decision is merely being preserved.

There is a false comfort in calling this stubbornness, and stubbornness sounds like a trait, one that belongs to certain people more than others. This mechanism is less flattering because it is more general. Once you have spent money, time, reputation or affection on a judgment, changing your mind appears to threaten all of it, and the earlier expenditure feels as though it must be redeemed by the next decision. Yet the past cannot be redeemed in that way. It is already past, and your next decision can only govern what remains available to you.

Markets make this arithmetic brutal, and a trader who paid more for a share than it can now be sold for may feel compelled to hold until the price returns to the earlier level. That earlier price has enormous emotional weight because it marks the point before the loss existed. Yet the market has no reason to care what was paid, and the relevant decision is not whether the old price was fair. It is whether holding the share now is justified by what can be known now. A person may choose to hold for sound reasons. He should not confuse the wish to get back to even with a reason.

You face similar arithmetic whenever an earlier cost becomes a command, and the course already completed, the money already paid, the years already given and the public commitment already made cannot tell you what the next month deserves. They may matter. They should be counted honestly. They should not be allowed to disguise the fact that you are making a fresh judgment in the present. A decision that was rational six months ago can be irrational now without proving that you were irrational six months ago. That sentence is hard to accept because it denies us the clean comfort of being either right all along or wrong all along, and life is usually less tidy.

Difficult work lies in identifying what would make a person revise a view before the pressure of revision arrives, and this is not the same as demanding certainty. Certainty cannot be awaited in most consequential parts of life. Nobody will know enough to remove all risk from a move, a relationship, a medical choice or a professional change, and the question is narrower. What evidence would count against the current position? What event would make continued commitment require a new explanation? If there is no answer, the position may be a preference that has borrowed the language of judgment.

That question can sound severe. It should. It asks you to make room for the possibility that your future self will be partial, afraid or proud. A person who sets a limit before the pressure begins is not confessing weakness. He is recognising a condition that applies to everyone: under pressure, your reasons can become difficult to separate from your desire for relief. A written rule, a trusted second reader, a date for reconsideration or a record of the original premise can restore some distance. None guarantees wisdom, and each makes it harder to glide from judgment into defence without noticing.

The aim is not to turn life into a series of rigid exits, and people who leave at the first discomfort do not possess superior judgment. Relationships need patience. Work requires persistence, and a project can look worst just before a necessary adjustment makes it better. There are times when the right response to adverse evidence is further inquiry, not retreat. A useful rule must be capable of being tested against reality, not used to flee it, and the opposite failure is just as common: a person calls every uncomfortable fact a reason for another look, then discovers that the additional inquiry has no end because its real purpose is to avoid a conclusion that would otherwise be unavoidable.

This is where the financial laboratory becomes revealing, and a market forces the conflict between flexibility and discipline into repeated view. If you refuse to sell because you want to remain open to new information, the price keeps supplying it. If you revise your plan every time the price changes, you may be calling a refusal to decide flexibility, and if you cling to the original plan regardless of what happens, you may be calling fear discipline. Labels are easy.

Everything depends on whether new information has a place in your reasoning that was available before you knew whether it would favour you. A chart pattern is a shape that traders believe may say something about the way a price is behaving, and backtesting means looking at how a stated strategy would have performed against past market data. Paper trading means applying a strategy in a simulated account. Each practice can be valuable because it gives a trader a way to look before acting with money, and each has limits. A pattern can be seen where none exists. Past results may not repeat, and a simulated loss does not test the same nerves as a real one. Still, the underlying impulse is sound: make the premise visible before the result makes a flattering account too tempting.

That impulse can be borrowed without a single market term. In a difficult conversation, write down what it is meant to accomplish and what will happen if it becomes abusive or circular. For an expensive commitment, state the conditions that would require reconsideration. Before lending money, decide what can be afforded never to recover, and before making a habit of postponing an appointment, ask what outcome would make the delay seem plainly unwise. These are not rules for a painless life. They are ways of refusing to let the eventual outcome be the first moment at which the decision is examined.

The author did not enter the account without resources, and four respected applications stood between a large market and his attention. They gave him filters, alerts, visual history and a direct route to an order. Those tools were not the missing element, and forty-seven years of professional life had also supplied experience in environments where decisions could be tested, explained and reviewed. That training did not make a loss impossible. It did make the failure to stop more difficult to explain away.

Experience had travelled, but its authority had not travelled with it into the private setting where the author alone decided whether a fact required an answer or merely another look at the screen. This gap matters because it is probably not his alone. A person may be excellent in a setting where work has consequences for other people and far less careful where nobody will examine the reasoning. Wise advice may be given to others and go unfollowed when the facts carry one's own name. Discipline may have been learned as a response to an institution, a deadline or a colleague, then mistaken for a permanent feature of character. When the structure falls away, the degree of reliance on it may become visible.

That discovery can be embarrassing. It can also be useful. If good judgment is partly supported by conditions outside you, then the response is not to demand a grander form of willpower. It is to build conditions that make self-examination more likely, and put the original reason in writing. Ask someone who has no stake in agreeing with you. Fix a time at which the decision must be reviewed, and separate the evidence from the story you are telling about the evidence. Make it possible for your future self to see what your earlier self actually believed.

Such measures can seem humble beside the confidence with which people usually speak about judgment. They are humble because judgment is fallible. They accept that you will want exceptions when an exception protects your pride. They accept that a live problem can make a prior agreement feel crude. They accept that your best intentions may be sincere while still being insufficient. There is nothing glamorous in this. There is also no reason to be ashamed of it, and the person who expects partiality is not less serious than the person who trusts instinct without examination. He has simply taken the future version of himself into account.

Pressure changes the reasons you can hear. It does not change the facts. You may be reading this while carrying a decision that has begun to acquire a number, even if the number is not money. It may be hours lost to an obligation that no longer has a purpose. It may be sleep lost to a worry you will not name. It may be the distance that has entered a relationship after too many carefully managed conversations. It may be a project kept alive by the fact that it has already consumed so much. You do not need to declare it a failure today. You do need to distinguish the fact itself from the explanation that lets you postpone responding to it. That distinction is the opening work, and a judgment deserves loyalty only while it can survive inspection. When it cannot, the next page begins with the question you have been finding ways not to ask.

## CHAPTER ONE

# Four Screens, No Decision

One morning, I opened four applications but did not look through them. Finviz was open. Trade Ideas was open. TradingView and thinkorswim offered their familiar invitation: see something, decide something, do something. I had bought each of them for a reason I could state plainly at the time. Finviz would narrow a market of thousands of tickers down to the small number that met conditions I had set myself. Trade Ideas would watch that narrower field while I was doing something else and alert me the moment it moved. TradingView would turn a rising or falling price into a shape a person could actually read, rather than a number that only told him where things stood at that instant. None of that was meant to produce excitement. It was meant to produce a decision I could defend, built on something visible rather than a feeling that the moment had arrived. That had been the whole idea behind the scanners from the start, to trade less on instinct and more on what the screen could actually show me. On this particular morning, I did not begin the usual work of arranging what I saw into a reason to act. I added instead. Over seventeen months, I had lost more than $20,000 scalping stocks during the day. Finviz cost $39.50 a month. Trade Ideas cost $254 a month. The pair came to $293.50 a month, roughly $4,990 across the period. The figures were not hard to find. Allowing them to mean one thing on the same desk took longer.

I qualified as a lawyer in Malawi in 1978, and served over the following decade as a state advocate, then principal state advocate, then chief state advocate. I later studied law again, was admitted to the Virginia bar in 1997, the Maryland bar in 1999, and the District of Columbia bar in 2005, and practised until I ceased in 2016. I am now a licensed Maryland realtor and a licensed Maryland mortgage broker. On that morning, those facts sat beside the loss without correcting it. That proximity matters because it removes a convenient explanation. A reader might prefer that I had entered this activity without training or professional habits, without experience of making decisions whose consequences did not disappear when the meeting ended. It would make the story far neater. It would also make the account entirely false.

The shape of that morning does not belong to markets. Everyone has a familiar activity that becomes strange when viewed from just outside it. You may notice it when the calendar repeats an appointment that no longer serves the purpose for which you first made it. You may notice it when a routine expense arrives. The amount is unchanged, but it has begun to describe a habit you no longer defend. The first useful distance is often this small. You stop treating the next instance as an isolated event and see the sequence that has been carrying you.

Suppose you drive a car whose engine has acquired a small, irregular sound. At first you turn the radio up. The sound disappears into the ordinary business of getting to work, collecting groceries, or arriving on time. A week later you hear it again, but you are late, so you give it a name that permits delay: nothing serious, probably weather, something to mention at the next service. You may read about the model, listen more closely at a red light, or ask someone who has owned a similar car. Each act can feel responsible. Yet the important fact is not how much attention you have paid. It is whether any observation would make you book the appointment. If every new sound merely becomes material for further watching, care has become a way of keeping the car on the road. The morning you decide to call the garage is not necessarily dramatic. It is the morning the noise stops being information about the next journey and becomes information about the vehicle itself.

The screens gave me a great deal of information, enough to make the question unavoidable. I had paid for access because I believed better sight would make me a better actor. That belief contains nothing foolish on its face. In real estate and mortgage work, information matters because a missing fact can change the decision before a person. In law, a fact omitted from a file can distort advice before anyone notices. More information does not guarantee a sound conclusion, but ignorance has never improved one.

No reader needs a brokerage account to know this pattern, because an ordinary routine can collect so many small permissions that it becomes an arrangement nobody deliberately chose, every step explainable by the circumstance of the day, while the completed sequence asks for a judgment no individual step was ever intended to provoke on its own. Once you have recognised that change in scale, the question is not whether you were foolish to take the earlier steps, because their reasonableness may be genuine, but whether you will continue treating yesterday's reason as sufficient evidence for tomorrow after the accumulated result has begun to answer a different question. Care begins when you permit the whole pattern to challenge the explanation that was adequate for a single instance, then decide that the next action must answer to the pattern rather than repeat the defence of what has already happened. The needed distance is not indifference to the past, nor a denial that you acted for reasons that once made sense. It is the discipline of allowing a repeated outcome to become evidence about the practice that produced it.

In that way, the screens gave me a respectable story about myself. No part of the exercise felt like guesswork. I was not treating the market as a casino in which enthusiasm could do the work of thought. Using tools, I watched activity. I treated my short-term decisions with what appeared to be more care than the person who simply pressed a button and hoped.

Care, though, has a way of becoming a word that ends an inquiry. Once a man calls himself careful, he can begin to treat the label as evidence. I want to be careful here: I am not saying the work was imaginary. Work differs from the thing it is meant to produce.

That morning did not reveal a single bad trade. It revealed that I could not name one. I do not remember the particulars of the trades that made up the loss. There are no tickers I can set down here, no dates, no sizes, no clean sequence in which a decision led to a result followed by a lesson followed obediently behind. That absence embarrassed me more than the number at first, and across years of legal practice I kept case files, because a professional file has a purpose beyond the memory of the person who made it. It records what was known and considered, then shows what was done while the matter was still alive. I cannot reconstruct the repeated decisions that formed the loss over those months.

Memory supplies impressions in place of a record. What memory preserves is the opening of screens.

With it comes the sense that something was about to happen, and that failing to act would itself be a mistake. I remember returning after a short holding period to another chance that seemed more urgent than the last. I do not remember enough to turn those impressions into a reliable account.

That is a limitation, not a pose. A reader is entitled to ask for the transaction that contains the whole error in miniature, the one moment with a before and an after. I cannot provide it. More precisely, I could provide a story shaped from the general feeling of the period, but it would acquire details in the telling that I do not possess.

This absence also closes another escape hatch. It would be comfortable to regard the loss as the product of one spectacular lapse, because a lapse has a beginning and an end, and this was not that kind of event. It was made from many trades, repeated sessions, each held for a short time. Its repetition helped prevent any one of them from receiving the attention the total now demands. A total loss can arrive with a false simplicity. It looks like a verdict. It is not a verdict, at least not by itself. It tells me that money left, but not what I told myself while it was leaving. No number discloses whether confidence moved me, or whether I acted from a conviction I had not taken the trouble to state aloud.

Still, it has one virtue. It refuses the consolations that a more elaborate account might offer. I cannot set the loss against a remembered triumph, because I do not have a faithful register of either. I cannot make the disappointing entries seem modest by selecting a dramatic winner from the same period. What remains is a plain amount and the fact that it accumulated while I believed I was engaged in a serious activity.

Greed will occur to some readers. That thought occurred to me at once. Greed is an efficient explanation because it carries its own punishment. It lets the observer remain outside the mechanism: a greedy man wants too much, so he loses what he deserves to lose. The word does not describe the atmosphere in which I worked, and an explanation that is morally satisfying can still be mechanically useless.

I did want to make money, and there is no cleaner way to say it, and no point pretending that the prospect of profit was incidental, yet wanting money is shared by people who never scalp a stock and by people who do it once and stop. It tells us almost nothing about why a person continues after the evidence has become unfriendly. Nor does the word careless settle the matter. Carelessness usually means failing to attend when attention was available. I attended. I paid for platforms and scanners, then returned for repeated sessions. The activity received time that I could have given elsewhere. Attending, however, is not the same as seeing the fact that deserves attention.

That distinction is unpleasant because it denies me a simple acquittal. Had I been merely careless, I could imagine a version of myself who became careful and escaped the problem. Each tool encouraged that fantasy because it suggested a further improvement in attention. Another view, another filter, another set of figures: each looked like an addition to diligence.

Diligence is real. A person who has not read the document is in a worse position than a person who has read it. A person who has not noticed the adverse authority, the authority that runs against the position being advanced, may make a claim that collapses on first contact. Training has taught me this often enough that I trust the lesson.

Diligence is not a solvent for every error. It can make an error more durable when the work is directed toward confirming a position rather than testing it, and a man may accumulate material in good faith and still select it with a purpose he has not admitted. With more work, he may give himself more credit for the conclusion he wanted before the work began. I do not mean that I sat at the screens scheming to deceive myself. That would again make the story too tidy. It would give deceit a clarity it seldom enjoys. Ordinary self-deceptions take a familiar form: I am preparing rather than acting blindly, and the statement can be true while leaving the central question untouched.

What mattered was not whether I knew enough about a stock at a given instant. I do not now pretend to know what would have counted as enough, because the decisions came and went too quickly for that question to receive an honest answer. Instead, I needed a way to recognise error while there was still something useful to do about it. Equipment was in front of me. No such method was available to me.

This is not an accusation against the equipment. Finviz did what Finviz was there to do, and Trade Ideas did what Trade Ideas was there to do. TradingView and thinkorswim were not withholding a private truth from me. They provided information in an accessible form. None had promised to substitute for the person using them.

It would also be unfair to make the screens villains because they now sit near an uncomfortable number. They did not call themselves wisdom. They did not ask me to confuse a fuller display with a better decision. My confusion belonged to me, though that puts it too strongly if it suggests one deliberate moment rather than a habit that developed without announcing itself. Professional habits can survive long after their setting has changed. I learned to look for what was missing, to notice a word that altered a sentence, and to hesitate before offering a conclusion with more confidence than the material could bear. Those habits were useful. They were not, however, a general licence to trust every conclusion produced by a mind that possesses them.

Speed created part of the difficulty. Intraday scalping offers very short holding periods and repeated chances to act. It narrows the interval between seeing and doing until a thought that has barely taken shape can feel like a decision. On the screens, urgency wore the clothing of information.

A person can be fully occupied in such an interval. He can move from comparison to reaction, then return to the next movement without pausing long enough to ask what would count as contrary evidence. Nothing forces the pause. There is no opposing advocate on the other side of the desk, no file that must be complete before it can go out, and no rule that requires a person to describe the weakness in his own view.

Rather than feeling reckless, the pace felt participatory, which is why the episode resists the usual language of addiction or thrill-seeking. Often I was intensely engaged. Engagement did not make the activity sound, and uninformed is another word that fails. I had access to information I did not have to seek by hand. I paid materially for some of it. I knew enough to understand that short-term trading involved uncertainty and that any apparent opportunity could disappear, and no one persuaded me that a scanner abolished risk.

Knowing that risk exists is not the same as allowing it to govern conduct. Most adults understand, in the abstract, that a plan can fail. Risk becomes useful only when it alters what they do while the plan is unfolding. An abstract warning is easy to preserve because it makes no demand at the moment action is most attractive.

Consider a repair in a home. You receive a quotation for work that seems manageable. Once the work has begun, something behind a wall or under a floor calls for more money. You may reasonably approve the first addition because leaving the work half done creates its own problem. A second addition follows. Now the original price feels important for reasons that have little to do with the remaining work. You have already endured disruption, made rooms unusable, and explained the project to people who visit. Each new decision may be defensible in isolation. You can ask for photographs, compare invoices, seek another opinion, and tell yourself that you are protecting what has already been spent. All of that may be careful. Still, there comes a point at which the question changes. It is no longer whether the next charge can be explained. It is whether the project, as it now exists, deserves another charge at all. If you cannot say what would make you stop, the original quotation has become an argument for continuing rather than a record of what has changed. The check is not whether you have been diligent. It is whether diligence still permits a different answer.

That is why the arithmetic on the morning mattered. The losses were not a theoretical danger I had agreed might occur. They had already accumulated during work that had seemed serious and purposeful. The figures offered no argument. They did not need one. They simply remained.

I found no dramatic revelation in the figures, and there was no theatrical disgust, no declaration that a former lawyer ought to have known better, and no relief in calling myself stupid. Stupidity is another escape hatch. It gives a clean separation between the person who made the error and the person reading about it. I do not think I was stupid. I do not say that in self-defence, and a stupid person is capable of losing money in precisely this way, but intelligence does not prevent it. Intelligence can supply explanations quickly, find distinctions that preserve a preferred position, and turn an uncomfortable fact into a problem that appears to require more research. It can be an excellent servant of delay.

Here the legal habit has an obvious attraction. A trained reader learns that first impressions are provisional, that a sentence can mean less than it appears to mean, and that the apparent answer may change after the relevant authority is checked. Those are good lessons. They also make it possible to keep an unwelcome conclusion pending for a very long time.

Pending sounds prudent. In some settings, it is prudent. A conclusion reached before the necessary material is available has no special claim to respect, and a lawyer who announces certainty before checking the authority is performing confidence rather than work. Trouble begins when postponement no longer serves inquiry and instead serves the position that inquiry has weakened.

I recognise now that I had many opportunities to use the vocabulary of caution without practising its substance. I could say that a result was not yet clear. I could tell myself that a short loss was merely a temporary fact. I could return to the screen because the next chance appeared to offer more information, when what it offered was another chance to defer an admission, and the word admission deserves its place here. It is not merely a statement of fact. To admit a mistake is to let the fact alter the standing of the person who made it, at least in his own eyes, and that alteration can feel larger than the mistake itself. A person may therefore resist the admission long after he has stopped resisting the evidence.

No reader needs my professional history to understand that resistance. You may have watched it in another person, particularly when the person had a reputation for being sound. You may have watched it in yourself, when the cost of saying plainly that something was wrong seemed greater than the cost of carrying it one more day. What recurs is not the thought that the position is correct, but that it is not yet necessary to concede.

I do not know exactly when that thought became operative for me. Missing records prevent the pleasing fiction of a precise point of origin. There were many trades and repeated sessions, and the condition I can describe is not a single choice but an accumulation of choices made under an interval too short for much inspection. That is as far as candour permits me to go.

Credentials do not cure the gap in the record. If anything, they sharpen it. The professional training behind them, and the licensed work that followed, place weight on information and disclosure. I let this period become an account I could not explain plainly, and that sentence might be read as a confession of hypocrisy. It is not, because hypocrisy requires a standard announced for others and knowingly withheld from oneself, and my difficulty is less flattering and more common. I believed standards of care belonged to the part of my life in which another person had a claim on my attention. I failed to notice how much I relied on that external claim.

When work involved a client or a transaction, the consequences had shape. Someone could ask what I had considered. Someone could require an explanation. The prospect of that question did not make me virtuous. It made certain omissions harder to maintain. Alone with a screen, I could be both the person advancing the position and the person deciding whether its weaknesses deserved to be heard.

This is a concession to the reader's first objection. Of course no professional training makes a person immune from loss, and no amount of care eliminates uncertainty. Anyone who says otherwise is selling a comfort rather than describing a condition of life. Uncertainty is not the same as helplessness, and the fact that an outcome cannot be guaranteed does not excuse refusing to recognise what the outcome is showing.

A second objection is fairer still, and intraday scalping may simply be a poor fit for the habits that had served me elsewhere, and that may be true. A poor fit does not explain why I remained in it through repeated sessions while the loss accumulated, or why the machinery of being well equipped made remaining feel like a responsible choice. Training is often described as if it were a possession, like a tool kept in a drawer, and that description flatters the trained person because it makes the benefit portable. In practice, training gives a person a setting with expectations and recognisable failures, but remove that setting and the possession may prove less complete than it felt.

In law, I learned to distinguish a holding from dicta. A holding is the part of a decision necessary to its result, and dicta are observations that may be illuminating but do not carry the same force. That distinction trained a useful suspicion of attractive language. A sentence could sound decisive and still fail to control the question at hand.

That habit did not become useless when I looked at a screen. It simply did not tell me what to do with a sequence of short-lived prompts to act. I could recognise that a display was not an argument. Yet a display could still move me faster than an argument would have done. A mind can know the category of a thing without resisting its effect.

I do not regard that as a defence. I regard it as a boundary on the defence that professional experience supplied. Someone who has spent years checking the support for a proposition may be less likely to believe an unsupported assertion. He is not thereby protected from acting before he has decided what proposition needs support. There is a related temptation to call the loss untrained behaviour, as though the years before the screens had simply vanished. They had not vanished. They appeared in a preference for paid information and the impulse to look again, especially when a decision could be tied to something observed. Even so, the training travelled with me, while its authority did not automatically travel with it.

That is a harder account because it leaves no external culprit and no easy corrective. I cannot say that a lack of knowledge led me into an activity for which knowledge would have been the cure. Nor can I say that carelessness produced a result that better organisation would reverse. I had organisation enough to make the activity feel official. I had knowledge enough to give each new piece of information a plausible place.

A man can make an activity official by surrounding it with apparatus. He can pay a monthly fee and arrange the visual field, then tell himself that preparation has become a property of the choice that follows. It has not. Preparation may improve a choice, but it does not inherit the choice's burden.

Any analogy to a file has limits. I do not want to force it. A file stays still long enough to be read, whereas the material before me in intraday trading did not. A file also exists for a defined matter, while the screen offered repeated matters that appeared and disappeared before one could decide whether they were matters at all. That difference was part of the arrangement. Nor were the losses proof that every act had been unsound. That claim would exceed what I know. It would turn the number into an authority it cannot be. Some decisions may have been reasonable and still lost, and some may have been poor and happened to work; I lack the detail to assign those labels honestly.

The inability to classify each decision does not entitle me to withhold judgment about the whole period. The pattern is plain enough for that. I spent a sustained period making many short-term trades, incurred a substantial loss, and cannot show how the process was being controlled. A careful man must not use the absence of complete proof as permission to ignore the proof that is available.

The available record is enough to make a narrower claim. No lack of alternatives pushed me into the activity, because I had work as a Maryland realtor and mortgage broker. Nor was I deprived of instruments, because four applications stood open that morning. Professional memory of how to test an assertion was also available to me. None of that stopped the repetition.

It would be easier to make the word failure carry the whole account, and failure names the outcome without making a demand on the observer. Refusal is the more exact word, or rather the quieter refusal to let an accumulating fact interrupt a method that still felt industrious. That kind of refusal can look remarkably like work until the arithmetic is placed on the desk. My stopping came on an ordinary morning, in the only way that now seems relevant. There was no outside event that forced the account open for inspection, and no one took the screens away. Nothing new appeared in the applications to settle the matter for me. I had the same instruments, the same capacity to search for one more reason, and the same ability to make a short interval feel like a complete consideration.

What changed was smaller than a revelation. I ceased treating the losses as information about the next trade and treated them as information about the activity itself. Once stated, the distinction is plain, though it was not plain while I was inside the repetition. A loss could always be folded into the next decision, and the total could not.

I closed nothing in the manner of a grand moral gesture. I stopped. The screens remained capable of offering the next thing to watch. I remained capable of finding a reason to watch it. The four open applications no longer looked like evidence of care. They looked like four windows through which a man had spent too long declining to see the same fact. When a repeated result changes the meaning of the activity, let the result govern the next decision.

## CHAPTER TWO

# A Careful Man

In 1978, qualifying as a lawyer promised a particular kind of safety. It was not safety from loss or error, because the law offers neither. It was safety from arriving at an answer by accident. Careful reading and controlled language, together with the habit of testing a proposition, promised conclusions better than those reached by confidence alone. It was a promise I had every reason to accept, and the promise was not empty. Legal education trains a person to slow the first movement of the mind, which is often the most flattering movement because it makes the answer appear at once. A proposition is placed before you, and the training asks what supports it and what limits it before considering the distinction that might deprive it of its apparent force. That way of thinking is not decoration.

A distinction between a holding and dicta makes the point. A holding is the part of a decision necessary to its result. Dicta are observations that may be useful or persuasive without doing that necessary work. Learning to separate the two is an early lesson in refusing to let a well-phrased sentence become more authoritative than it is. At first, this can feel unnecessarily fussy. A person outside the profession may see two sentences that point in the same direction and wonder why one receives so much attention while the other does not. That difference becomes clear when a conclusion depends on it, while language may carry an air of certainty even when its legal force lies elsewhere.

Beyond the courtroom, the habit teaches that confidence does not improve an assertion, nor does an example automatically become a rule. A careful reader asks who said it and under what authority. Those questions can save a person from a great deal of foolishness. I do not say this as an admirer looking backward for a reason to feel superior. I say it because the training worked on me. It made me less impressed by the first answer. It made me aware that a conclusion had a burden, and that its burden did not disappear because I preferred the conclusion.

There is a physical side to this kind of thinking: you read a sentence again, notice the word that changes its reach, or see the fact that prevents a broad statement from applying as broadly as it first appeared, perhaps because the small word turns out to define the whole proposition before you. Then you return to the proposition and find that you have not answered it after all. Its point is not delay for its own sake. It is to avoid calling an unfinished thought a result. That is a better way to live in many situations. It prevents the loudest person in the room from acquiring authority merely through volume. It gives an unpopular fact a route back into the discussion. It permits a person to say, without embarrassment, that he does not yet know.

Part of the education was learning that not knowing until authority is checked is not a failure of nerve. It is a condition of speaking responsibly when the answer will guide someone else's conduct. A lawyer who turns uncertainty into certainty before doing the work may comfort a listener, but the comfort rests on something he has not earned. Law also directs attention toward adverse authority, the authority that supports the other side or weakens the position you want to advance. It is not a decorative act of fairness. It is a recognition that a conclusion is only as reliable as its treatment of the best material that runs against it.

Although the discipline sounds obvious in a quiet room, it asks a person to work against his immediate interest by locating the strongest reason his view may fail. He may find that reason inconvenient, and its inconvenience does not reduce its force. In professional work, that habit had a place and a consequence. Professional work did not make me immune to preferring my own view. No training manages that. It did require me to understand that preference was not a substitute for support. My mind could lean in one direction, while the material pointed in another.

There is considerable reassurance in such a system, and the rules of the work create a place for doubt without requiring a person to become vague. You can state a position firmly and still identify its weakness. You can advise action while acknowledging that a contrary authority may affect the result. Candour does not prevent a conclusion. It makes the conclusion answerable, and that answerability was not an abstract benefit. It supplied a form of resistance when I was tempted by an easy reading. A file with an opposing argument, plus the expectation of explanation, made certain shortcuts harder to take. I want to be careful here: they did not make shortcuts impossible. They did not make every conclusion right. They made the ground beneath a conclusion visible enough for another person to question it.

This is one reason legal reasoning earns trust: it does not claim to remove uncertainty, but gives uncertainty a method that requires a person to keep looking until he can state both what he knows and what remains unresolved, rather than using confidence as a substitute for the material. A person learns to identify the material fact, the fact that affects the outcome, and to distinguish it from a fact that may be striking but changes nothing. Materiality is a modest word for a large restraint. It tells the reader not to carry every available fact into the conclusion merely because it exists. Some facts belong in the file and some bear on the decision. The art lies partly in knowing the difference. That art is not infallible, but it improves with practice because it is repeatedly exposed to correction.

Correction is an important part of the bargain. A lawyer learns from a rejected distinction or an apparently decisive fact that proves narrower. Professional practice provides many ways for a conclusion to meet resistance before it becomes too settled in the person who formed it. A person trained this way develops a reasonable confidence, not because the method has removed the possibility of error, but because it has forced him repeatedly to see how a plausible conclusion can fail when a neglected distinction or fact finally comes into view. It is confidence in a procedure: read, check, compare, reconsider, then state what the available material permits. Although the procedure is imperfect, it is plainly better than deciding by instinct and later finding language to make the instinct sound considered.

That last comparison matters. Legal reasoning is often criticised for allowing a skilled person to dress up a preferred answer in technical terms. That criticism has force. A trained mind can indeed build a handsome argument around a conclusion it wanted before it began, and legal language can obscure that fact more effectively than ordinary speech.

The criticism stops too early if it treats the training as mere ornament. The same discipline that permits an argument also gives another person tools to expose its weakness. Holding and dicta, material fact, along with disclosure and adverse authority, are handles by which a claim can be pulled apart. A system that permits contest is not therefore a system that guarantees truth. It is a system that makes a false certainty work harder for its place, and that is a genuine achievement. A trained person learns, or ought to learn, that even a conclusion reached after effort remains open to a missed objection.

That word carries weight here, though I do not use it as a sermon. People fail at standards they recognise, but a visible standard has a force that private preference lacks. It can be invoked by someone who has no interest in protecting the conclusion you would most like to preserve. Such work creates a particular professional self-image. It is not entirely vanity. A person who has repeatedly taken a claim apart and accounted for what resists it has a basis for trusting his own habits. He has seen those habits prevent avoidable mistakes.

I had such a basis. I qualified as a lawyer in Malawi in 1978, was later admitted to the District of Columbia, Virginia, and Maryland bars, and practised law for decades before ceasing to practise in 2016. My confidence was not borrowed from a title. It came from repeatedly seeing careful work produce a better account than haste would have produced. There is no reason to pretend that this confidence was irrational, and the lawyer who checks the authority before making a claim will generally give better advice than the lawyer who does not. A lawyer who notices the material fact will generally reach a more useful conclusion than one distracted by a vivid irrelevance. A profession that rewards these habits has earned some faith in them.

Danger begins when earned faith becomes a passport. A person with a reliable method in one setting can begin to trust not merely the method but his own possession of it. The distinction appears small in language but large in consequence. Method depends on conditions, while self-regard travels without asking whether those conditions are present. For a time, the familiar habits remain visible. He still notices ambiguity, still has an instinct for the question that has not been answered. Still finds simple certainty unpersuasive. Because the habits remain, he assumes the warrant for confidence remains as well.

That assumption does not announce itself as arrogance. It can arrive as a quiet competence, even as modesty. A man may think, quite sincerely, that he is not rushing because he knows how dangerous rushing can be. He may not notice that he has entered a situation whose pace has already decided what his familiar caution can accomplish.

If you think of yourself as careful, you know the satisfaction of asking the extra question. Suppose a repair in your home begins with a written price. You save the estimate, read the scope, and make sure the work starts only after you understand it. Then the first unexpected problem appears behind a wall. A second follows. You ask for an explanation each time. Photographs are taken. Then you compare the invoice to the original estimate. Those are the actions of a prudent person. Yet carefulness has a limit that is easy to miss: it can verify each new charge while leaving the larger project unexamined. The question that protects you changes as the cost grows. At first it is whether the new work is necessary. Later it is whether continuing the whole project is still the best use of your money, time, and attention. A person who has done thorough checking can be especially slow to ask that later question, because the evidence of his care is everywhere. The invoices are orderly. Those stored photographs help. Your original decision still feels present. None of that answers whether the conditions that justified it remain.

Legal method depends on an interval: there must be time to read what bears on the point, examine a contrary view, revise a sentence, and allow an overlooked fact to alter what will be said before the sentence does its work in the world. An interval does not guarantee wisdom. Nothing does. Without it the method becomes a set of gestures performed after the decision has already been made. In a file, the interval is built into the object, and the papers wait. An authority found later can alter an earlier opinion or require a sentence to be redrawn before anyone relies on it. Even an urgent matter gives the worker some relation to time other than immediate reaction.

That distinction is easy to miss because quickness also has a respectable appearance. A person who sees the point rapidly may look more capable than a person who asks for time, and in some matters, rapid comprehension is plainly useful. Understanding a question quickly is not the same as having completed the work needed to answer it. You can see the temptation in your own decisions. A familiar problem arrives, and the resemblance to something already known feels like knowledge of the answer. It may be knowledge. It may also be the first resemblance only, the one that hides the different fact on which the result will actually turn.

Legal training tries to interrupt that moment. It says that the fact which looks familiar may not be material, and the fact which looks slight may control. It asks the reader to hold an answer provisionally long enough for the shape of the problem to become less flattering. This is a costly habit in time, yet it earns its keep when a premature answer would mislead someone who relies on it, and the habit also has an emotional benefit. If a person has followed a method with care, he can accept a result that disappoints him without believing he has been personally defeated by it. He did what the material allowed, and the result may be unwelcome, but the process has given him grounds to distinguish an adverse outcome from a careless one.

That distinction is not an excuse for indifference, and a lawyer cannot hide behind procedure when the procedure was used to avoid the inconvenient fact. A well-conducted process matters because outcomes are often not fully within the actor's control. Training teaches a person to judge conduct by what was known and done at the time, not only by the result later observed. That point becomes distorted when it leaves the setting that made it useful. Outside a professional structure, a person can invoke process without being able to show the process. He can call himself careful without producing the adverse material he considered. He can describe an outcome as unfortunate while leaving untouched the question of whether he had built any route by which unwelcome evidence could change his course.

None of this was in my mind when I began trading intraday. That transfer was subtler than any deliberate claim of entitlement. Years spent treating attention as a virtue made attention itself seem conclusive, and there was attention. Finviz and Trade Ideas sat alongside TradingView and thinkorswim. I opened the screens and watched them repeatedly. Those facts were easy to mistake for proof that I was doing the intellectual equivalent of checking the authority.

They were not proof, and a display can provide information without providing a process for deciding what the information means. It can make an observer more alert while leaving the observer no more capable of naming the fact that would require him to stop. Movement of attention can feel like reasoning, particularly when it is fast and the available information is abundant. I want to be careful here: I want to make a concession before drawing the line too sharply. The tools were not false. It is sensible for someone making a decision to seek useful information. A screen can show something that would otherwise be missed, just as a well-kept file can preserve a fact that memory has neglected. No tool has a professional duty to challenge the person who uses it.

No screen asked me to identify the authority against my next decision, and no screen required disclosure of the strongest reason not to act. It showed what it was designed to show. I supplied the importance. An opposing voice seemed absent by design because the activity was private, and that privacy was part of its attraction. A private decision can be perfectly sound without any external supervision. The point is not that a person needs supervision to think. The point is that someone accustomed to external checks may mistake the confidence produced by those checks for a personal quality that persists when the checks are gone.

That transfer is especially seductive because it contains a truth. I had learned habits worth carrying: respect for material fact and caution about first impressions, plus a willingness to qualify a weak conclusion. Those habits did not become worthless merely because I used them in another setting. What failed was the inference drawn from their presence. I saw evidence of familiar habits and assumed they were doing familiar work. More precisely, I assumed I was entitled to the confidence those habits had earned in a setting that asked much more of them, and the confidence crossed the boundary, and its warrant remained behind.

That phrase may sound harsher than necessary, or rather less fair than the training deserves. After all, people transfer skills every day. Civilisation would be poor if every capacity were confined to its first use. A reader who has learned to read closely in one occupation may indeed read more closely in another. Transfer is not entitlement, and a resemblance between tasks is not proof that the old safeguards have come along. This distinction mattered because I had a history that supported my self-assessment. I was not a man who had never been required to consider the other side. I was not a man who regarded precision as an inconvenience. I had spent years in an occupation where an unexamined conclusion could do harm, then I worked as a licensed Maryland realtor and licensed Maryland mortgage broker, occupations in which information can also carry obligations that ask a person to distinguish possessing a fact from allowing the fact to affect what he tells another person, a difference too easy to lose sight of in a private account.

Those facts could reasonably have made me cautious. They could not make me entirely safe. This is the part a careful man resists, because safety is what carefulness has seemed to provide all along. When a method repeatedly keeps a person from making obvious errors, he begins to imagine that he has acquired a general resistance to error itself.

He has not acquired any such resistance. He has acquired a practice that works only where external challenge supports it. Remove those conditions and the practice may survive as manner. It may still look exactly like care. It may still feel exactly like care. Its familiar appearance is precisely what makes the loss of function hard to notice.

There is a difference between knowing how to inspect a proposition and having enough time to inspect the proposition before acting, and there is a difference between recognising a weak inference and feeling the need to act before a weak inference has been named. A person may preserve every intellectual virtue he values and still enter a system designed to keep those virtues from influencing the moment that matters. One claim is not a criticism of legal reasoning. It acknowledges its proper strength. Legal reasoning is good at forcing a conclusion to disclose its basis. It is good at making a person live with the contrary material that basis cannot absorb. Its power lies partly in slowness, because slowness permits a claim to be met by more than the appetite that produced it.

A second claim is more troubling: a trained person may overlook the loss of those conditions because he recognises his own gestures of care. He sees himself taking care, yet does not notice that the object will not wait and that the chance to act has already passed. This is not a plea for untrained innocence, and ignorance does not become a virtue because knowledge can overreach. Nor does it follow that a careful person should avoid every domain in which the old rules do not apply. What follows is narrower and less comforting: confidence needs an address.

A person may know where it was earned. He may even be able to list the habits that earned it. What he cannot assume is that the confidence will know where it belongs once he carries it elsewhere. It does not carry a map.

You can see the same error in a task with none of the dignity of a profession. A person notices a change in his health that is probably harmless, then decides to wait a few weeks before making an appointment. He does not ignore it. Reading about the symptom, he remembers a similar episode and watches for changes. He may be trying to avoid needless alarm. The careful story becomes more persuasive with every day of observation. Yet observation has no value if it has not been joined to a condition for acting. If the symptom worsens, you may say you will call. With no change, you may say you will wait. A brief improvement may become permission to wait longer. The person is not foolish. He is trying to make a measured decision. What he may fail to notice is that each possible result has been given the same answer: more waiting. Care does not consist in accumulating reasons to defer. It consists in deciding, before comfort enters the analysis, what evidence will require a change of course.

There is another reason the training deserves generosity. It does not merely teach scepticism. It teaches a person when scepticism has done enough work to permit a conclusion. Endless hesitation is no virtue. A professional cannot respond to every question by discovering a further uncertainty and leaving the other person to bear it alone.

This matters especially to the reader who prides himself on not being impulsive, because you may be more willing than most people to gather information, acknowledge complexity, and delay a decision until you can defend it, all of which are admirable habits until they become a way of avoiding the point at which a decision must be revised or made. You may be the person friends call before signing an agreement, changing jobs, or confronting an awkward problem, precisely because you can identify qualifications that others have missed. Such praise can make caution feel like character rather than a practice that depends on time, resistance, and a willingness to let evidence close off a preferred path. The discipline is not to become less careful. It is to ask whether your careful procedures still contain a moment at which unwelcome evidence can do its work.

A lawyer must often advise before perfect knowledge is available. Professional work identifies what is known and what remains uncertain, then explains how uncertainty bears on the available choices. That is demanding because it resists two easy postures at once: false certainty and evasive caution. Each protects the adviser more readily than it serves the person asking for help.

Often, the best professional answer is not a firm one. It may be conditional, because the facts themselves are conditional. It may say that one conclusion follows if a material fact is established and another follows if it is not. That is not weakness in the speaker. It is accuracy in the relation between language and evidence.

Such accuracy has a moral force, although moral language can make the work sound more elevated than it feels at a desk. Much of the time it is plain effort. At a desk, you look again. Then you put the attractive point beside the point that undermines it. At last, you remove a sentence that exceeds what the material will support.

Those acts are not dramatic, but they are how a conclusion becomes dependable enough for another person to use. They also teach a practical humility. A writer discovers that the sentence he first liked most may be least able to survive contact with the available authority. Repeated exposure to that discovery can improve a person's judgment.

It improved mine in the setting where I learned it. I had ample reason to believe that precision was not merely an ornament of professional life. Precision prevented an opinion from promising more than it could deliver. It allowed an uncertainty to appear before it caused damage rather than after.

Confidence formed by that experience is not the same as vanity. Vanity says that the person is right because he is the person speaking. By confidence I mean something more defensible: practices that expose error make it less likely that I will carry an error forward unnoticed. That conclusion is reasonable within the conditions that made the practices real.

It is also incomplete. An error can escape not because a person has abandoned his method but because the thing before him does not permit the method to operate. A method has a tempo as well as a set of rules. If the tempo changes, the rules may be present only as intentions.

Consider the act of checking. In the professional setting, checking is a completed action with an object. You compare authority to the proposition and alter the conclusion if the comparison requires it. Its value lies not in the word checking but in the time and resistance the sequence contains.

Outside that setting, the word can become loose. A person can claim to have checked because something moved or confirmed a feeling he already had. He may have looked hard. Considerable time may have been spent. He has not necessarily performed the act for which the professional word stands.

This is not a matter of calling ordinary behaviour professional language in order to make it respectable. It is a matter of failing to notice when the language has become a substitute for the act. A sharper professional vocabulary can make that substitute more available.

He has many accurate words. He may deploy them inaccurately on himself.

I had not stopped valuing evidence when I began trading. I had stopped practising law in 2016, but the habits of mind were not put away with the work. They seemed like an ordinary part of how I recognised a serious question. My problem was recognising seriousness in the apparatus before asking whether it had created room for the habits I valued.

Those instruments rewarded a certain resemblance. Finviz and Trade Ideas, along with TradingView and thinkorswim, presented more than a bare invitation to guess. They gave the activity the visible features of examination: information before me, with categories and recurring opportunities to compare. A man accustomed to labouring over material can feel at home among such features.

Feeling at home is not a minor thing. It lowers the guard that an unfamiliar activity might otherwise provoke. If the setting feels familiar enough, the person need not announce to himself that he is crossing a boundary. He can tell himself that he is applying a known competence, when in fact he is entering a different arrangement that has borrowed some of the same furniture.

That resemblance had another effect. It made the old confidence feel conscientious rather than expansive. I did not need to believe I possessed special insight. I needed only to believe that a man trained to gather material and avoid impulsive conclusions was entitled to treat his attention as dependable. That belief was modest in tone and large in reach.

A reader may think this description gives training too much power, as though a professional habit could explain every decision a person makes years later. It cannot. People act for several reasons, and no single explanation accounts for every decision in an extended period. Training supplied a ready explanation for why I felt entitled to continue looking, and entitlement is often enough to keep a questionable activity from receiving the scrutiny it needs.

My point is not that I failed to understand risk. Legal work does not teach a person how to eliminate risk, and neither does real estate or mortgage work. It teaches that risk must be described with enough candour that someone can act with their eyes open. In a private account, however, I could treat my own awareness of risk as though it satisfied the whole obligation.

Awareness is a poor substitute for a process of response. A person can know that a position is exposed and do nothing different because the knowledge has not been connected to a rule for acting. In professional work, the possibility that another person will ask what you did with the fact gives the fact a kind of weight. Alone, one can keep the fact present without letting it decide anything.

That is why carefulness can become a hazard. A careless person may be alarmed by his own lack of preparation. A careful person, having done some preparation, may feel protected from the need for alarm. Preparation is not imaginary, though the protection may be.

I am not arguing that the careful person is worse off. That would be another form of self-dramatisation. It would misdescribe the training. Care improves decisions where its methods can be used. Real danger is more ordinary: a useful strength can make a person slow to recognise the moment when it no longer reaches the task before him.

In 1978, I received training that taught me to distrust a conclusion that had not met resistance. I had good reason to prize that training in the years that followed. Much later, sitting before moving screens, I mistook the familiarity of my own careful manner for evidence that the work which had once justified it was still being done. That confidence had left the room in which it was earned. It was still wearing its name. When you rely on carefulness, test whether the conditions that make care effective are still present.

## CHAPTER THREE

# Adverse Authority

Across years of legal practice, I spent part of almost every serious piece of work looking for the material that could hurt it. The name for it was adverse authority: a rule, decision, or principle pointing against the position I had been asked to advance. It was not a decorative exercise in professional modesty. I had to find the strongest answer before somebody else found it and used it without mercy. A reader unfamiliar with law may imagine that lawyers merely collect support for their side because that is how advocacy is usually shown. In the practice I knew, collecting support was only half the assignment. The other half resisted me.

Adverse authority is easier to explain than to practise. If I made an argument, I had to identify the authority that made it doubtful, weaker, or wrong. I then had to deal with it honestly enough that the person deciding the question could see the problem without assistance from my opponent. This did not mean abandoning every position with a difficulty in it. It meant I could not hide the difficulty and call the result analysis. The distinction has teeth under pressure. No one enjoys the first encounter with a useful authority that damages his own case. The immediate sensation is irritation, followed by an effort to narrow the damage. Then comes the wish that the text had said something slightly different and left the argument intact. I remember that sequence as a professional reflex rather than a moral failing peculiar to anyone else. A person who has spent days building an argument does not greet its best refutation like a long-lost friend. His first impulse is to reach for a distinction.

There are times when the distinction is real. Language has limits, facts matter, and a rule applied in one setting may not govern another. In that work I learned that careful distinction is not evasion when it identifies a difference that actually changes the result. I also learned how easily the mind can turn a small difference into an escape hatch. A difference that bears no weight can suddenly seem decisive because the alternative is conceding that one has built too much on the wrong ground. The professional task was to tell those two moments apart.

That task had a form. I had to read the unfavourable text closely enough to state it fairly, not merely closely enough to find an adjective that could be pressed into service. I had to ask what the other side would say about it when they had the benefit of distance from my commitment. I had to decide whether it controlled, could be distinguished, or required a different argument altogether. The sequence was not glamorous, but it gave thought a structure. It made denial expensive before denial could do much damage. That was the point.

In ordinary speech, people use the word authority to mean a person who speaks with confidence. In law it means something less flattering and more useful: a source that limits what you may plausibly say. It does not care how elegant your theory is or how long you have believed it. It sits there, already written, and forces an encounter with what will not fit, and that is why trained lawyers can become tiresome in conversation. We have spent too long being interrupted by texts.

The interruption matters more than the answer, and before I could persuade anyone that my position was sound, I had to show that I had not missed what made it unsound. The obligation made a claim upon my attention at exactly the point where my attention wanted to leave. It did not ask whether I felt ready for correction. It required the work before I could comfortably proceed. In that limited setting, the rule was a small machine for producing candour.

I want to be careful here: the machine did not make anyone pure, and a professional rule cannot abolish self-interest. It does not reliably make a person generous in private life. What it can do is insert an unwelcome question into a process before the process has hardened. Its question is simple: what is the best thing that can be said against me? Asked early enough, it changes the shape of the preparation. Asked late, it may only record the shape of a mistake. My practice taught me that adverse authority has a peculiar advantage over general advice about open-mindedness, and open-mindedness asks a committed person to become less committed by an act of will. Adverse authority asks him to find a particular text, read it, describe its force, and explain why it does or does not decide the issue. One request depends on temperament, and the other creates a job. Given a job, most trained people will do more than they do when invited merely to improve themselves.

There was no mystery about why the job had to be required. Left to myself, I could always find another supporting source, another possible interpretation, another sentence worth refining. Each offered the decent appearance of work. None required me to approach the argument from the side where it was most vulnerable, and research can be a refuge from thought when the researcher controls the direction. The shelves are full of places to hide. That was no accident.

You do not need to be a lawyer to see the missing protection. In ordinary life, nobody makes you seek the fact that would make your preferred plan harder to defend. You decide whether to look, when to look, and how much weight to give what you find. That freedom can feel mature. It can also leave you alone with the part of your mind that wants the plan to survive.

Suppose you are buying a house that feels immediately right. You can picture where the furniture will go. The price seems manageable, and every visit makes the decision feel more settled. Someone mentions a survey, the document that shows the actual boundaries and features of the land. You know it might reveal an encroaching fence, a shared drive, or a portion of the garden that is not what you assumed. The information is available, but it is inconvenient. You decide not to obtain it because the sale already feels far along and because a result that complicates the purchase would make you start again. When you decide that a survey can wait because you have told family you have found the house you want and because starting again feels worse than proceeding, a missing document begins to support the conclusion you preferred: it is never asked to contradict you while the seller waits for an answer and while every pleasant feature of the house gives your choice another reason to seem settled. Nothing about the choice need feel reckless when the rooms feel right and the contract seems ready and each harmless detail is allowed to crowd out the single unexamined fact that could require you to withdraw before the purchase settles into a story you must defend even when its basis is uncertain to everyone else.

Nothing forces you to seek the document. The absence of it begins to feel like evidence that no problem exists. Later, a boundary question arises. The surprise is not that the survey was wrong. It is that the fact that could have undone the decision was never invited into it. You did not need bad intentions to avoid the survey. You needed only a reason to keep the pleasant version of the purchase intact.

Consider a smaller form of the same habit. Suppose your car has made an intermittent noise for weeks. You lower the radio when it happens, listen closely, then turn the volume back up. When you take the car in for routine service, you tell yourself that the noise has stopped or that it would be embarrassing to describe something you cannot reproduce. The question you avoid is simple: could this become unsafe or expensive if I leave it alone? You do not ask because you suspect the answer may disrupt your plans and cost more than you want to spend. That is not recklessness in the dramatic sense. It is the ordinary wish to postpone a fact that might require action. The car does not need to fail for the omission to matter. Once you notice that you were reluctant to ask, you have learned something important about the decision already under way.

A warning deserves a hearing before it becomes a bill. A rule against concealment changes the incentives, and once I knew that an adverse point had to be faced, finding it early became preferable to finding it late. Early discovery left room to adjust the argument or to advise against pressing it. Late discovery created embarrassment, wasted effort, and the prospect of appearing less careful than I wished to appear. The rule did not make the unwelcome source welcome. It made ignoring it a worse choice. Every hour spent polishing an argument that the source could undo was an hour spent constructing an embarrassment. Someone else had no obligation to spare my feelings. He might expose the problem in a few damaging sentences and leave a record of how long I had protected the argument from the page that should have changed my mind.

That is a modest achievement, though it is not a small one, and much of adult error persists because nobody has given the person making it a reason to seek the disconfirming fact before it becomes unavoidable. We praise independence, then leave people alone with the evidence that supports their first view. We praise confidence, then treat visible reconsideration as a weakness, and under those conditions, a person does not need to be vain to become enclosed. He needs only to be busy with his own affairs. Self-protection begins there.

In the work I did, the duty also disciplined language, and if I described an opposing authority carelessly, I increased my own risk. Anyone on the other side could point to the text, and the decision-maker could read it. Precision was not a virtue displayed for applause. It was a protection against being caught making a statement that the record would not bear. I learned to separate what I wanted an authority to mean from what it actually said. That separation is one of the few forms of self-control that can be practised on paper.

Paper has an advantage over the mind, and a sentence written by someone else will remain where it is while you dislike it. It will not soften because you have found a more comforting explanation. It will not praise your persistence. You can read around it for an afternoon, but you cannot make it disappear by rereading your preferred passage. Facts can be equally obstinate, of course, but authority has the special annoyance of carrying a reasoned voice. Usually, the first defence against adverse authority is verbal. I would call the unfavourable source broad language or a special setting. I might describe it as an imperfect fit, an old expression, or an unnecessary observation. At times, all of that was accurate. More precisely, it was accurate often enough to make the habit dangerous, and a lawyer who never distinguishes anything is not doing the work, but a lawyer who can distinguish everything has ceased to notice the difference between analysis and escape. Experience did not remove that danger. It gave me better names for it.

Another form of defence works through time. A person tells himself he will return to the difficulty after finishing the more urgent work. He places the source in a folder, marks a page, saves a note, and feels the relief of having acknowledged it without yet confronting it. I saw this manoeuvre in myself because I had the same human equipment as everyone else, and delay can be sensible, and delay can also turn a live objection into an item of furniture. By the time it is revisited, too much has been built around it.

A third defence arises in the social setting. When people have heard an argument repeated with confidence, the speaker begins to hear their attention as confirmation. A room can give a weak idea a temporary appearance of solidity simply by allowing it to proceed uninterrupted. No one need agree for this to happen. Silence can perform the work of assent, as can politeness, fatigue, or a desire to finish a meeting. An adverse authority has the useful impoliteness of not caring whether the room is tired.

Professional practice offered fewer consolations than people suppose. I was not rewarded for finding a problem with an argument in the same way I was rewarded for making an argument sound persuasive, and the adverse work slowed me down, complicated conversations, and occasionally narrowed what could responsibly be claimed. It could feel like taking money from one's own pocket, even when the actual consequence was only less comfortable language. Still, the work protected the claim from a more serious failure: meeting its strongest objection unprepared.

There is a difference between an argument with no weakness and an argument whose weakness has been examined, and the first may be an illusion created by incomplete research. An argument of the second sort may still lose, but it has been made with open eyes. In practice, that difference affected every recommendation I could responsibly make. I did not need certainty before I spoke; I needed to know what stood in the way. They are plainly not the same standard.

People outside professional settings often believe that confidence comes from having no contrary evidence. I found that a different confidence was available after the contrary evidence had been located and weighed. It was quieter. It gave less pleasure in the moment. It did not permit grand declarations. It did allow a person to say, with some basis, that he had looked where the trouble was likely to be. For a long time, I mistook that hard-earned habit for a permanent feature of my own mind. It was not permanent. It was situational. I had a rule, a reader who expected compliance, a professional setting in which omission could be exposed, and a body of work that rewarded the search when it was done properly. Remove those conditions and the habit did not stand upright by itself. I do not say this to diminish the training. I say it because the training worked through arrangements as much as through character.

That concession is harder for a trained person to make than it sounds. We like to think that repeated professional conduct becomes an internal possession, something carried intact from one room to another. Some of that professional conduct does become internal. I still notice loose language, unsupported certainty, and the odd comfort people take in an unexamined assumption, but noticing is not the same as submitting oneself to correction. What troubled me was whether I looked for what I did not want to find when no one required the search.

I did not always do so, and that sentence has less drama than I once expected, but it has more consequence. In a personal decision, there was no opposing advocate preparing a response, no fixed record waiting to contradict a convenient version, and no decision-maker whose patience I had to respect. There was only the position I wanted to keep and the information I could arrange around it, and the absence of a rule felt like freedom. In truth, it was closer to permission. No one told me to stop.

A person can conduct a surprisingly persuasive private hearing. He knows which facts make him look sensible because he has selected them himself. He knows the context that excuses the doubtful part because he supplies the context. He can postpone every hostile question without appearing to postpone anything, since no deadline exists except the one he dislikes. He can also mistake the fluency of his own explanation for its truth. None of that, plainly, amounts to madness. It is more ordinary. It is the ordinary advantage of being both advocate and audience.

What I lacked outside practice was not information, and in recent months I have had no difficulty locating reasons for and against a view whenever I decide that locating them is the task. Harder still is deciding who begins that task. In law, the answer was built into the role, and in private life, a person ordinarily begins the search only after discomfort has already become strong enough to overcome his preference. By then he has often spent a long time arguing alone.

Markets gave this problem a particularly clean form. With screens, scanners, charts, plus a habit of looking, I could find information at speed. I could find an interpretation faster still. No one required me to set beside a proposed trade the strongest reason not to make it. No one required me to write down the condition that would prove my view wrong. Nor was a candid account required after the position had closed. Abundance was what the equipment supplied. An adverse advocate was not. Each new movement invited an interpretation, then carried it along before it had met a contrary case. The activity continually supplied reasons to look without requiring a reason to stop. I was not forced to decide whether a proposed trade had survived its strongest objection; I could always go on gathering material.

What I can see is the missing procedure, and when I worked with a difficult legal position, I had methods for bringing the unwelcome material forward. I deliberately read against the desired answer. I tried to state the contrary point in language its defender would recognise. I asked whether my response actually met it, or merely changed the subject. At a trading screen, I too often behaved as though rapid access to confirmation was the same thing as a process for contradiction.

That comparison is not exact. I do not want to force it into exactness. A legal argument differs from a short-lived market position in its evidence, timing, and consequences. A rule that makes sense in one may be awkward or useless in the other. The difference does not erase the underlying pattern. When I wanted an answer badly, I was more willing to assemble support than to appoint an opponent.

I had spent a career learning the practical value of an opponent, and the best opposing argument is not an insult to your position. It is a test of the claim you are asking others, or yourself, to carry. If the claim survives, it is stronger for having been tested, and if it does not survive, the failure has arrived before the costs have multiplied. This is not an uplifting lesson. It is an economy of damage.

Outside a courtroom, people often reserve this work for a crisis. They seek disconfirming evidence when a decision has begun to fail publicly. They may seek it when a relationship has become difficult to defend or when a number refuses to be explained. By then, the search comes with humiliation attached. Such evidence has to overcome not only the original belief but the labour already spent protecting it. An early adverse question is cheaper because it has not yet acquired a personal biography.

I have come to think that the most useful part of professional restraint is not restraint at all. It is the creation of a second voice with standing to interrupt the first, and in practice, the record supplied that voice. A rule supplied it, and another advocate supplied it. Finally, the person charged with deciding supplied it. Those arrangements did not eliminate error, but they prevented one person's preference from occupying the whole room. When the room belongs only to you, the furniture moves easily, and a missed warning becomes a fact you had considered, and a prediction becomes a plan. A plan becomes evidence of competence because you made it with care, and this process can happen without a lie ever being spoken aloud. By emphasis, not merely deletion, the mind performs its edits. It places the agreeable material near the centre and makes the rest look peripheral.

I recognise that description because I once regarded myself as unusually protected from it. Training had taught me how arguments fail, and experience had shown me that the first account of a problem is rarely the final one. I knew, in the abstract, that confidence often outruns support. Knowledge of a tendency is not immunity from it. It can become a further reason for believing oneself exempt. That is one of the less charming forms of professional vanity.

A strong professional rule can therefore produce two contrary effects. It can make a person more careful where the rule applies. It can make him overestimate his carefulness where it does not, and the first effect is real and deserves respect. Success within a structured setting then feels like evidence about the self rather than evidence about the structure. I had learned a method, but I credited the method's results to an enduring trait.

I do not mean that nobody voluntarily seeks the case against himself. Some people do, especially after experience has made them wary of their first enthusiasm. Others appoint a sceptical friend, keep a written record, or delay a decision on purpose. Those devices are sensible substitutes for a rule. They require a person to build by choice the constraint professional life once imposed. Most of us discover the need for one only after we have seen what absence permits.

Candour is often made to sound ceremonial. In practice, it meant saying the part that made my position less attractive in the immediate moment. It meant resisting the temptation to offer a technically accurate description that left the listener with a materially false impression. It meant admitting when a source created a problem I could not solve by force of tone. Candour did not always make a conversation pleasant. It made the conversation usable.

There is a private version of candour. I had treated it as optional for too long. It begins when a person stops asking whether he can defend a decision and asks what would make him withdraw it, and the first question has almost no limit. Given time, intelligence, and a desire to prevail, a person can defend nearly anything to himself. By contrast, the second question creates a boundary. It asks for a fact, a condition, or a result that would end the argument. Even a stated boundary is not a guarantee. Even after naming a condition, a committed person can redescribe it when it arrives. He can say the result was temporary, the evidence incomplete, the timing unfortunate, or the standard unfairly strict. I have seen all those moves in the general run of human reasoning. I have made versions of them myself. Still, a written boundary leaves a trace of the earlier mind. It gives the later mind something harder to revise without admitting the revision.

The loss of that trace matters greatly. Without a record, each new moment can pretend to be the first. The person holding a position need not acknowledge how often the same warning has appeared. He can also ignore how many explanations were offered or how much confidence accompanied the earlier view. He experiences only the present version, which is always capable of sounding reasonable. Repetition becomes invisible when no one keeps count.

This is why I cannot take much comfort from the fact that I had professional-grade tools on my screens. Finviz and Trade Ideas, alongside TradingView and thinkorswim, bought access rather than correction, and information arrived in quantity. What did not arrive was an obligation to make the hostile case before acting. A scanner may reveal movement. It cannot compel a concession. The screen made no objection.

Beyond the markets, that same distinction persists. A person can have reports, advisers, history, data, plus the benefit of prior mistakes. He can use all of it to defend a conclusion already chosen. More information makes this easier when nobody has assigned it a contrary role. It gives the advocate within us a larger library. Without becoming more honest, the thought merely becomes better furnished.

In my years of practice, I came to trust procedures that made the difficult work ordinary. A checklist can be dull, but dullness has its uses when excitement is trying to narrow the field of vision, and a requirement to put the adverse point in writing can feel mechanical, yet it requires an act that private confidence prefers to avoid. Repetition can turn candour into a habit of attention, though that puts it too strongly. Repetition can at least make concealment less effortless.

What no procedure can do is concede for the person using it. Even when the adverse source is found and accurately described, a person may treat it as a minor inconvenience despite its actual force. The reader can still deceive himself. I knew that limitation in practice; I know it now. Rules change the odds. They do not transfer responsibility away from the person who wants the result. Even so, I miss the external demand. I miss the point at which the work stopped being a matter of preference and became a condition of proceeding, and in a life without that demand, I can feel an argument harden because I have not given it a competent adversary. I can feel the small relief of looking only at what supports the next action. Relief is often the first payment made to a defended position.

An adverse authority does not arrive to humiliate the person who has found it. Properly used, it is a warning before the wall, not a judgment after the collision. I had understood that throughout my professional life. My surprise is not that I forgot the principle. It is that I expected the principle to operate without the machinery that had made it real. I had mistaken an enforced habit for a private instinct.

No remedy lies in staging a little courtroom in every ordinary decision. That would be exhausting and absurd, and nor do I think a person can live by arguing himself out of every preference, hope, or attachment. Some decisions require action before full assurance is available. Something smaller and less comfortable is at issue: when a decision begins to matter, someone needs the job of stating what could make it wrong.

For a long time, I treated the opposing view as a burden carried for the benefit of a decision-maker. I now see that it was also a service performed for the person making the argument. It kept me from becoming entirely dependent on the version of events that suited me. It did not guarantee a good result. No available method could do that for anyone. Nothing in it flattered me. But it gave error an earlier chance to introduce itself.

A contrary source often becomes useful earlier than pride permits. Before a commitment has become public, the cost of changing course is usually small. Before money, time, or reputation attaches itself to a view, a correction may feel almost ordinary. Later, the same correction can look like a confession about the person who resisted it. I saw that difference repeatedly in professional life. Nothing had changed in the substance of the adverse point, but the price of admitting it had.

That price explains why intelligence does not solve the problem, and intelligence gives a person more ways to make a weak position sound provisional rather than weak. It finds context and ambiguity and the plausible exception. Those capacities are valuable when they expose a crude argument. They become dangerous when they merely delay the moment of acknowledgment. I have no reason to think myself exempt from the appeal of a clever qualification. A clever qualification can feel like movement when it is only a better furnished form of standing still. I used to think that the central professional virtue was the ability to make a forceful argument. There is a place for that ability, and a person who cannot put a coherent case is of limited use to anyone who needs help. Yet force without a contrary check becomes pressure. For the fluent advocate, language can readily outrun its underlying support. I learned to value the moment before force, when the argument had to endure a reading that was not trying to help it. That moment was less visible, but it did more of the protective work.

A private decision can borrow the outward manner of that work without receiving its benefit. I can make notes, open sources, or mark a warning while arranging the exercise so the conclusion remains untouched. Form is not the same as submission. Only when contrary material is allowed to alter the possible answer does the discipline begin. I want to be cautious about the word discipline, because it suggests sternness for its own sake. What I mean is a willingness to give unwelcome evidence the same right to affect the decision as welcome evidence.

In practice, the duty also required a degree of imagination. I had to anticipate how a person who disagreed with me would read the authorities I preferred, and that was not empathy in the sentimental sense. It was an effort to enter an opposing line of reasoning far enough to see its strongest construction, and doing that made me less certain of some arguments and more confident in others. It also reduced the temptation to treat disagreement as proof of bad faith. An opponent could be wrong and still see something I had missed.

Difficulties arise with the private equivalent because the opponent has no independent voice. If I supply the argument against myself, I also control both its timing and its strength. I can make it sound foolish, then congratulate myself for having considered it. This is one reason a written question is better than a vague intention. It can ask, in plain terms, what evidence would make me stop. It can remain unchanged after I have begun to prefer continuation. Although the question cannot force an answer, it can make avoidance more visible.

I do not claim that every important mistake arises from ignored contrary evidence. Some outcomes are bad because the world changes, because information was unavailable, or because an honest choice carried risk that later materialised, and no amount of internal cross-examination abolishes uncertainty. The claim I make is narrower than that. When the adverse case was available and a person declined to make it, he has removed one of the few brakes that operate before consequence supplies its own lesson. That is not certainty. It is a chance to pay less for being wrong.

Now the role of compulsion looks different to me. A compulsory rule does not merely threaten a penalty for omission. It relieves the individual of having to decide, at the exact moment commitment makes the decision unwelcome, whether he will seek the evidence that may undo him. Before commitment has done its work, the rule has decided in advance. It makes room for an earlier, less invested self to govern the later self. There is nothing heroic about that arrangement. It is prudent because the later self has reasons the earlier self cannot share.

A person who has never worked under such a requirement may find it fussy. I understand the reaction, and from outside, the careful presentation of the opposing position can look like a ritual performed by people who enjoy obstacles. From inside, it is closer to checking a door before leaving the house. Neither safety nor interest in the journey is guaranteed by the check. It prevents a certain kind of avoidable trouble, which is reason enough to value it.

What stays with me is not a memorable argument, since I am not telling any, but the repeated physical act of turning a page toward the material I would rather not find. That act was small and often tedious. It was also a refusal to let preference decide what counted as relevant. I had been trained to make that turn because the role required it. Alone at a screen, with no one waiting for the adverse page, I discovered how much of my apparent independence had depended upon being obliged to look.

On the screen, the colours change quickly and the argument arrives dressed as urgency. Before the full sentence has formed, the hand moves. There is no clerk or opposing advocate. No marked page sits on a desk asking to be read again. There is only a bright assertion, then another, plus the small blank space where the adverse authority ought to have been. Before you act on a decision that matters, give the unwelcome fact a place to change it.

CHAPTER FOUR

# The Client Who Wants Certainty

Across those years of practice, I rarely met a client who came to me chiefly for a range of possible outcomes. People wanted to know what would happen. They wanted the answer to arrive without much visible hesitation. They were not foolish for wanting this. A difficult situation can make uncertainty feel like a personal insult, as though the professional has withheld the one service for which he was engaged. Usually, the first demand is not for an argument but for relief.

I understood the desire. Before a person seeks advice, he has often spent considerable time alone with a question that has no settled answer. He has heard contrary opinions, read too much, or replayed a conversation until every phrase seems to contain a warning. By the time he asks for help, he may not be asking for more information. He may be asking someone else to stop the movement of his own mind. That is a serious need, even when no honest adviser can meet it fully. In my practice, the honest answer was ordinarily a range. Facts could develop in more than one direction. Another person could behave in ways no one could predict. A decision-maker could see a point differently from the way I saw it. A professional could explain the relevant considerations and identify the more likely paths. He could not turn likelihood into a promise without changing the nature of what he knew. Still, a range has a way of sounding evasive to someone who has come for a verdict. Certainty is what he came to buy.

Difficulty begins in the gap between what can be said truthfully and what the listener can bear to hear. A client may understand in the abstract that no adviser controls the future. He may still listen for a firm conclusion in every careful qualification, then feel disappointed when the qualification remains. This is not necessarily manipulation. It is the ordinary wish to be rid of a burden. Nobody enjoys paying for an expert answer that ends with conditions. Conditions, however, were the answer. They were not a professional habit added to make speech cautious. They described the part of reality that remained outside anyone's command. When I said that an outcome depended on evidence, timing, conduct, or a later decision, I was naming obstacles that already stood there. I was not placing them between myself and confidence. A person seeking certainty can hear this as a failure of nerve. I came to see it as a form of respect.

Respect does not always feel respectful, and a qualified answer asks the anxious person to carry some of the uncertainty that he hoped to hand over at the door. It denies him the clean emotional transaction he imagined: he asks, I tell, and the future becomes manageable. Instead, he leaves with a better account of the risk and still has to decide what to do, and that can make the adviser look less useful than the person who speaks with serene certainty. Confidence has a commercial advantage over candour. It makes the speaker look useful at once.

I want to be careful here: a client does not always ask for certainty in so many words. Often he asks whether his position is good or whether he should worry. He may ask whether a feared result is likely or whether a choice will solve the problem. These are reasonable questions. Pressure appears in the pause after a careful answer, when it becomes clear that the person is waiting for the sentence that will cancel the rest. An adviser who recognises that pause has reached the point of danger.

Such danger is not usually an outright falsehood, and few professionals begin by deciding to deceive a person who has trusted them. The slide is smaller and more understandable. An estimate becomes a reassurance. A reassurance becomes an expectation. An expectation begins to sound like a commitment. Each step can be defended in isolation by the professional who wants to help or the client who wants to be spared the burden of choosing. Together, they create a version of the future that no responsible person had the power to offer. I learned to notice how much language can do before anyone has stated a lie, and a phrase such as probably fine may be heard as fine. A tentative assessment can arrive as a promise if it is spoken warmly enough. Even a careful explanation can be remembered later only for its most comforting clause, and the professional cannot control every recollection, but he can control the temptation to make a difficult message easier by making it firmer than the facts permit. That temptation is strongest when the other person needs relief badly.

There is a professional pleasure in being the one who can settle a room, and people become quiet when someone who appears to know more begins to speak. Their attention confirms the authority of the role, and the role can confirm the authority of the speaker. In practice, I had to watch that feeling because it made a neat answer more attractive than an accurate one, and the neat answer gives the professional a moment of gratitude. By contrast, an accurate answer may give him only a longer conversation.

Longer conversations are not failures. They are what occurs when a person must be helped to understand uncertainty rather than merely medicated with certainty. I do not mean that an adviser should drown people in every remote possibility. That would be self-protection dressed as thoroughness. It would leave the person no wiser than before, and the task is to identify the contingencies that genuinely affect the decision and explain their force plainly. It is work, not a disclaimer. The distinction matters. In my experience, people can absorb bad news more readily than vague news, and bad news has an edge. It lets the listener begin to adjust, however reluctantly, because he can locate the thing that has happened. Vagueness leaves him waiting for a blow that has not yet landed, and for that reason, a professional may be tempted to convert uncertainty into a negative prediction simply to give it shape. That too is a misuse of authority.

Accordingly, an honest range had to be narrow enough to guide and wide enough to be true. It required me to say what was known, what remained uncertain, plus what later fact would change my estimate. The sentence may sound simple, but it asks the adviser to resist several pleasures: appearing decisive, ending anxiety, and being remembered as reassuring. None is wicked. All can distort advice.

A client will sometimes press because he believes the professional knows more than he is saying, and often the belief is understandable. Expertise does mean that the professional sees patterns a layperson cannot yet see. He may be able to say that one course appears safer than another. There is a difference between seeing more and seeing enough to abolish risk. I had to keep that difference alive in my own language. Without it, knowledge becomes a costume for certainty. A client also has a part in this exchange. He may invite the professional to take over responsibility for a choice that remains his. If the adviser gives a confident answer, the client can act with less awareness of his own participation. Later, if the outcome disappoints, the certainty can be remembered as something supplied from outside, and that does not make the client dishonest. It shows why certainty is so attractive: it can move the burden of deciding onto someone else.

A good adviser cannot accept that burden simply because it is offered. He can explain, recommend, warn, or help the person see consequences. He cannot make the person's choice disappear by covering it with professional language. In practice, I found that the clearest advice often returned a portion of responsibility to the person who wanted to give it away, and this was not a rebuke. Or rather, it was a reminder that an adviser can share a decision without owning its future.

That reminder can feel unsatisfying at the time. A person comes to a professional precisely because he hopes not to carry the whole problem by himself, and there is no kindness in announcing that he is on his own. Better is companionship without impersonation: I can walk through the reasons with you, but I cannot become you at the moment of choice. That distinction preserves both usefulness and truth.

You have probably been the person who wants the answer to come without conditions. The wish is strongest when delay feels costly. You do not want a lecture about the limits of knowledge. You want someone to tell you which way to turn so that you can stop carrying the whole decision by yourself.

Suppose a leak appears over the kitchen ceiling a week before people are due to visit. You call a roofer because you want one answer: will the repair be finished before they arrive? The roofer can see the damaged area, but not every layer beneath it. A delivery may be late. Rain may interrupt the work. You hear the qualifications as obstacles because you have already planned around a firm date. The sentence you want is, "Yes, it will be done." Once you have arranged meals and travel and a room full of visitors around a promised repair date, every caveat can sound like a professional escape even when it is simply the accurate description of a job whose hidden parts no one has yet been able to inspect properly. If the roofer says it, your relief is immediate. You may stop arranging a backup plan. You may even hear the answer as a guarantee, although the conditions remain outside anyone's control. Your demand for certainty is understandable. It is also an invitation for another person to make the future sound cleaner than it is. A useful answer would tell you what can be done now, what could delay it, and what you should do if the delay occurs. That answer gives you work. It does not give you the relief you came to buy.

You may also be the person on the other side of that call. Perhaps a colleague asks whether a new hire will work out, or a friend asks whether changing jobs will solve a problem. You have an impression. You may even have good reasons for it. The other person is tired of weighing the choice and keeps returning to the same question. A measured answer keeps the discussion alive, while a firm answer ends it. You say, “It will be fine," because you want to be helpful and because you want the person before you to feel less distressed. If you tell your friend that the new job will certainly solve the difficulty because they are exhausted and because you want your care for them to have a useful shape, you may mistake the relief in their face for proof that your prediction has become more reliable than it was five minutes earlier. Nothing about the sentence feels cruel. You have changed your limited view into a confidence the evidence does not support. If events go badly, you may remember the careful reservations that were present in your mind. The listener will remember the sentence that allowed action to feel safe. You do not need professional authority to create this problem. You need only another person's discomfort and a wish to bring it to an end.

The firmer answer is often the easier one. I sometimes saw impatience with that distinction. I understood it. A person with a problem wants a line to stand on, while the professional keeps pointing to ground that may shift, and a range seems like an evasion when the listener's need is immediate. A line drawn too firmly can become a trap for both people. One party relies on it, and the adviser begins to defend it, and reality gets the last word. Professional failure does not often announce itself with dramatic intent. More often it starts with a sentence spoken a little too smoothly, and the adviser has made the client less anxious, the client has become more trusting, and everyone in the room prefers the new arrangement to the harder truth. Nothing appears wrong. Then a later fact arrives and reveals that the comfort was purchased by leaving something out.

I had learned, over years of practice, to distrust the sentence that produced immediate relief. Immediate relief is not proof of error, of course, and a careful answer can genuinely clarify a situation and remove a fear that had no basis. Relief can also show that I have told a person exactly what he wished to hear. That distinction depends on the work done before the sentence, not on the expression that follows it. There was a simple test available to me, and could I say, in plain terms, what might make my estimate wrong? If I could not name such a condition, I was probably offering confidence rather than advice. A range without reasons is evasive, but an estimate without a boundary is a performance. I did not always enjoy the test. It prevented the satisfying finish that both parties sometimes wanted.

When a professional first states an uncertainty, the client may hear a limitation in the professional. On a second hearing, he may recognise a limitation in the situation. By the third, if the explanation has been clear, he may begin to understand the point of the advice. Patience is needed here, though not the kind that congratulates itself for being patient. An adviser has to remain present while the person discovers that no one can make the uncertainty disappear.

This is where professional candour becomes difficult, and candour is not merely disclosure of a bad fact. It is the refusal to use one's superior access to information as a means of purchasing trust with a confidence one has not earned. A person who knows more can sound more certain than he is, and the listener may not notice the difference. Only the professional is required to notice it.

In law, I learned that a client can hear a prediction as an undertaking, even when the prediction was offered with qualifications. That fact made precision more than a matter of style. It affected the way I prepared a conversation, the way I answered a direct question, and the way I described the remaining risk. I had to assume that the strongest phrase in my answer might outlast the rest. Such an assumption is not pessimism. It is prudent attention to how people listen.

This work does not burden everyone evenly, and a client who is calm and informed may receive a range as useful information. A client under pressure may treat the same range as intolerable. No professional can solve that difference merely by softening the truth. He can alter the pace, choose clearer language, and make sure the person has understood what was said. He cannot replace a difficult reality with a more agreeable one simply because the person before him is frightened. I do not say this to praise professionals as stoics. We have our own appetite for reassurance. A client's need to hear certainty meets the adviser's wish to be seen as capable, and the two wishes can reinforce each other with alarming speed. One person asks to be told that the future is manageable, and the other discovers that he enjoys being the person who can say so. That is the compact to watch. It is easy to condemn the professional who exploits that compact cynically. Cynicism makes a clean villain, and clean villains spare the rest of us from looking at ordinary motives, and more commonly, the professional wants to help. He also wants the client to leave satisfied, to think well of the consultation, and to return if another difficulty appears. Those wishes are not corrupt by themselves. They become dangerous when they decide the content of the advice.

I want to correct an overstatement, and there is nothing wrong with reassurance when reassurance has a foundation. A person may be worried about a danger that the known facts do not support, and the professional can properly say so. Trouble begins when reassurance substitutes for the work of identifying what is known and what is not, then the tone has become the evidence. Tone is a poor witness. It cannot carry the weight of a fact.

A careful adviser must make peace with being disappointing. That is not the same as becoming cold or obscure. It means accepting that a person may leave less pleased because he has been told what he cannot yet know. Avoiding that disappointment is powerfully attractive because it feels humane. False firmness does not spare the client from uncertainty. It postpones the moment when uncertainty becomes undeniable.

Over time, I knew the sound of a question that was really a request for permission. What the client asked was what would happen, but he often meant that he wanted someone to authorise the choice already forming in his mind, and sometimes the right response was to say that the choice carried a risk he could not transfer. Sometimes the answer was that more information was needed. Either response could feel like withholding help, though it was the only form of help I trusted.

This may sound severe, though that puts the matter too starkly. I do not think it is severe to decline a power you do not possess. It is more severe to take it, perform it briefly, and leave another person with the cost when the performance ends. Professional authority is borrowed from a role, and a role does not enlarge the facts. It gives the speaker a duty to treat the facts more carefully than a casual observer would. That duty becomes most visible when the answer remains incomplete.

A range is not the absence of an answer. It is an answer that keeps its connection to the conditions that make it true. If conditions change, the estimate changes, and that is not inconsistency but accuracy. People often resent this because they hear a change in estimate as a change in character. They imagine that a competent person would have known from the beginning. No competent person knows what has not yet happened. I had to say versions of that without sounding as though I were hiding behind it. A professional cannot repeat that the future is uncertain as a substitute for preparation. He has to show what he considered, why one possibility carries more weight than another, and where the limits of the assessment lie. That range has to come from work. Otherwise it is only fog. An adviser has offered no guidance at all. One reason clients seek professionals in the first place is this: they do not need an adviser to tell them that anything could happen. They need help sorting what is material from what is merely imaginable. In my practice, material meant information likely to affect a decision, and the term was useful because it imposed a question on the adviser: would this fact change what a reasonable person does next? That is a question with consequences.

I found that the material fact is often the fact people most wish to soften. It may not decide the entire matter, but it prevents the easy conclusion. An adviser who leaves it unspoken has made the choice look cleaner than it is. An adviser who buries it in a flood of detail has done nearly the same thing, and disclosure is not accomplished merely by making a fact available somewhere. A person has to be able to see its force.

This is not a lesson about perfect communication. I cannot recall every conversation from practice. I would distrust anyone who claimed such a record from memory alone. I know I sometimes found better language after a conversation had ended. I know there were occasions when a client heard a sentence differently from the way I intended it. Part of the work is accepting the limit: people do not receive words as they leave your mouth.

A professional response to that limit is not to abandon precision. It is to make precision more active.

I learned to ask whether the listener understood the contingency, not merely whether I had spoken it. I learned to distinguish a nod from comprehension. I learned that a person can repeat the comforting part of an explanation while missing the condition attached to it. None of this creates certainty, but it does reduce the chance that reassurance will masquerade as advice.

All of that knowledge should have made me a difficult customer of certainty. It did not. When I began trading intraday, I did not sit across a desk from someone offering an estimate. I sat at a desk in Maryland with screens giving me movement, signals, plus the appearance of a continuous answer. The market did not speak in sentences, which made it easier for me to supply them myself. I became, in effect, my own client and my own adviser. That arrangement gave me every advantage I had spent years trying to prevent in professional conversations. I knew what answer I wanted. I could choose the information that seemed to support it. I could make the qualifying language disappear before anyone else heard it, and no client interrupted to ask what might make my view wrong. No adviser had to explain the range. Both the person who wanted certainty and the person tempted to provide it occupied the same chair.

I had spent a career resisting a client's wish to turn an estimate into a guarantee, and at a trading screen, I began to search for signals that would let me feel the guarantee without ever naming it. That is the reversal I find hardest to excuse. I knew the difference between evidence and reassurance. I knew how a tentative answer can become fixed in the listener's mind. I permitted a changing display to do the work of a confident professional voice. Speed in intraday trading made the mistake easier to miss, and an estimate in practice might be tested over days or longer, giving language time to reveal whether it had been too firm. A screen offers a new fact almost immediately. Each movement can feel like confirmation, contradiction, or the beginning of a rescue, and there is little silence in which to recognise that the original question was unanswerable. A display supplies attention faster than reflection can organise it.

I had Finviz, Trade Ideas, TradingView, and thinkorswim open in the general run of those months. The paid services made it possible to find more, see more, and react sooner. What they did not do was tell me when I had turned a possibility into a promise. A tool cannot refuse the assurance its user is determined to extract from it.

The arrangement has a dry quality that I cannot improve by describing it. The subscriptions were not the cause of the loss. They were part of the apparatus through which I hoped information would relieve me of having to tolerate uncertainty. Their real cost lay in the story they allowed me to tell about continued attention.

That hope is not foolish in the way I once might have called it foolish. Better information can improve a decision, and a careful tool can make a hidden fact visible or a pattern easier to notice. I do not blame the tools. I have no basis for saying they failed to provide what they offered. My problem was the private use of information as reassurance. I treated access as though it were an undertaking about the result. In practice, I would have recognised the manoeuvre immediately if someone else had made it. A client who tells himself that an adviser gave certainty when the adviser gave only a range is not necessarily lying. He may have heard the part that answered his fear. I did something similar with the market, except that I supplied both the qualified assessment and the confident memory of it. There was no second person to correct the record.

No neat parable emerges from the repeated sessions or the feeling that the next piece of information was needed. I will not manufacture one from general impressions. A polished account would explain too much. It would leave the pressure of the activity looking cleaner than it was.

At the screens, abundance made a fresh reassurance possible at every turn. I could move from one signal to the next without asking whether it contradicted the estimate that had justified the action. A fresh display made a fresh reassurance possible. No client would have accepted from me the level of explanation I accepted from myself. If I had told a person that the basis for an important recommendation rested only on a succession of fast impressions, he would have been entitled to feel poorly served. I did not apply that standard at my own desk. I was not merely more forgiving of myself. I was spared the ordinary friction of being answerable to another person.

Here again, I want to qualify the comparison. Markets are not client matters. No professional consultation is the same as an intraday decision made by one person at a screen. The risks, timing, and evidence differ. The appetite for certainty travels readily between settings. I had learned its sound when it arrived in another person's voice. I failed to recognise it when it began speaking with mine.

My failure was not wanting an answer. Everyone wants an answer when a choice is costly and the available information points in several directions, and the failure was that I mistook the tools of analysis for a source of assurance. I treated the existence of more data as though it reduced the need to ask what could undo my view. Instead, it gave me more material with which to calm myself before acting. A client who wants certainty is asking the professional to close the interval between doubt and action. I had been trained to keep that interval open long enough for material facts to appear, and on the screen, I wanted it closed. I wanted a signal to settle the matter quickly enough that the anxious part of the decision would not have to be endured. A more immediate signal always seemed more persuasive.

I do not know whether a formal rule imposed on my trading would have changed the result. It may have become another ritual that I learned to satisfy without learning from it. I cannot honestly claim a procedure I never used would have saved me. What I can say is that I removed the practices through which I had once kept reassurance from passing itself off as advice. I left the desire for certainty alone with the means to manufacture it.

Professional temptation to firm up an estimate is not confined to the professions. It appears whenever someone is asked for a judgment but fears that a conditional answer will look weak. Parents, managers, advisers, friends, plus people alone with a decision can all feel it. At first, it may arise from kindness, efficiency, or fear of being thought indecisive. It ends with a statement that has outrun the evidence.

You may recognise the client in yourself before you recognise the professional. You may ask someone who knows more to tell you that the troublesome possibility can be ignored. You may call this request for guidance. It may be partly that. Notice the moment when guidance would no longer satisfy you unless it removed responsibility. That is where certainty stops being information and becomes an anaesthetic.

Harder is the professional recognition. You may be the person whose confidence lets another person act too easily, or the person who supplies himself with the same confidence in private, and the wish to be useful can make a plain uncertainty feel like a failure of service. It is not. A true range may disappoint, but it leaves the person with a chance to decide in the world as it is.

I am writing this only months after the losses stopped, so I do not have a clean ending to offer. I still feel the pull of a sentence that would make a difficult choice simple. I still notice how quickly a confident voice, whether mine or someone else's, can make an uncertain position feel briefly settled. Knowing the mechanism is not the same as becoming free of it. It may only make the next reassurance sound less innocent.

A client who wants certainty does not necessarily want to be misled. Usually, he wants the ambiguity taken out of a decision that already feels too large, and that wish deserves sympathy. The responding professional has to supply something more difficult than reassurance: a way of acting without pretending that action has abolished risk. It is less satisfying than a prediction, and far more demanding than a disclaimer.

In my practice, I found that the useful conversation often began after the client had stopped pressing for the impossible answer. Once the need for a guarantee had been named, a person could sometimes ask a better question. A first question is what I can control. Next comes the question of missing information. Then I ask what consequence follows if the unfavourable possibility occurs. Those questions do not calm anyone immediately. They turn anxiety into work. Work is often the only honest form of relief available.

There is an irony here. A person who insists on certainty may believe he is demanding a higher standard from the professional, and in fact, he may be asking the professional to lower the standard of truth so that the future will sound simpler. An adviser who resists can appear less expert precisely because he has taken the limits of his expertise seriously. I learned to regard that appearance as part of the cost of doing the work properly.

I did not carry that lesson intact into my own decisions. This is not a confession of ignorance. It is an admission that I knew how certainty is manufactured in language, then allowed a screen plus my own impatience to manufacture it without language. Because it was less explicit, the certainty felt less accountable. No promise was spoken. The promise still governed the next action.

A range leaves room for correction. A certainty, once it has been accepted, begins demanding loyalty, and the person who has received it invests not only in the predicted result but in the person who supplied it. When that person is oneself, the investment can become almost invisible. I was not defending a formal prediction after every trade. I was defending the capacity to believe that the next display could settle what had remained unsettled. That capacity was expensive.

At a desk, certainty has a posture. It leans slightly forward, points to the brightest item on the screen, then speaks before the conditions have been named. The qualified answer is slower. It keeps a hand on the page where the troublesome fact remains visible. I have spent enough time on both sides of that desk to know which voice is more welcome, plus which one leaves the room quieter after it has gone. When someone asks you for certainty, name what remains unknown before your confidence makes it disappear.

## CHAPTER FIVE

# Two Licences and a Duty to Disclose

A licence is an odd thing to carry into ordinary life. It permits work that affects another person while making clear that the work is not entirely yours to define. I hold two Maryland licences now, one as a realtor and one as a mortgage broker, and each rests on the same uncomfortable proposition: when your work gives you information another person needs, you may have to offer it before you know whether offering it will cost you the business rather than retaining it in private until convenience has passed. That proposition is easy to praise at a distance. It becomes difficult at the moment an offer seems likely, a borrower seems ready, or a conversation has finally begun to move without resistance. A fact that would slow the matter down is often the fact a professional most wants to postpone, and a rule earns its place there. It asks for candour at the point where private preference would prefer another minute, another call, or a hope that someone else will raise the subject first.

Maryland real-estate rules use the language of a material fact, and in ordinary terms, a material fact is one relating to a property that could matter to a person deciding what to do. It is not every rumour, passing preference, or private impression, and a licensee who knows such a fact, or should know it through the work, may not quietly leave it outside the discussion. Silence can have the practical effect of a false answer when the silence keeps a person from making a choice with the relevant information. Professional duties are bounded by relevance and knowledge. No one can reveal every fact in the world, nor should a buyer be buried under a list so long that the important item disappears. Recognising when a detail has crossed from background into a fact that bears on the decision takes care, because that line will not always announce itself. It still has to be considered.

Representation has a similar purpose, and a person considering a property needs to know whom the licensee represents before mistaking a helpful conversation for a different loyalty. Agency disclosure belongs early because timing determines whether the information can still be used, and courtesy is not representation. A clear explanation of the relationship gives you a fairer sense of where advice, confidentiality, and advocacy actually run. Mortgage work places the same concern in numbers, and a borrower sees a proposed loan as an answer to a pressing practical question about payment and timing. A mortgage professional sees terms, charges, rate features, plus conditions in a more articulated form. That gap does not prove that the borrower is careless. It is built into a transaction in which one person encounters the structure more often than the other.

For a loan, the documents are not incidental. They are where the proposal becomes legible. Proposed terms and charges need to be set out early enough for the borrower to consider them, and later disclosures show the transaction in its closing form, allowing comparison with what was first presented. A figure offered only in reassuring conversation is not much help. You need a form you can read after the reassuring voice has gone.

Suppose you hire someone to repair a persistent leak at home, and the first visit produces a modest quote and a calm explanation. Work begins. Once a wall is opened, the person doing the work sees that the original plan will not solve the problem without more expense and more disruption. At that point, you need more than continued activity in the next room. You need to know what has changed, what it may cost, and what choices remain before the repair goes so far that stopping feels impossible. Delivering that news may be unpleasant for the contractor. You may dislike receiving it. Neither discomfort changes the usefulness of the moment. If the revised information arrives only after a larger bill has become unavoidable, the formal statement of the new price has missed the practical purpose of telling you. No difficult fact becomes less relevant because everyone wants the day to proceed smoothly.

Timing changes the substance of disclosure. Private life offers fewer formal protections. Suppose a person has agreed to help a friend make a decision that will affect them both, perhaps a move, a shared expense, or a commitment of time. Soon, that person begins to see a problem the friend has not seen, perhaps a cost left unmentioned, a limitation on availability, or a serious doubt about the plan. Nothing outside the relationship may require it to be stated. The moment can be dismissed as poor. The concern may disappear. Perhaps the friend will raise the point if it matters. Yet every hour of silence lets the arrangement gather weight. Plans are made. Other options are declined. The friend becomes more invested in the picture the first person has helped to sustain. When the concern is finally mentioned, the words may be accurate while the timing has stripped them of much of their use. No lie may have been told. Still, the friend has been allowed to decide inside a picture known to be incomplete. Later, the silence may be explained as an effort to avoid alarm before a solution was found. That explanation can be sincere, yet it still leaves the friend carrying a cost created by the timing of the silence. A shared decision calls for enough candour that the other person can decide whether the uncertainty is acceptable before preparations have become obligations and before a change of mind looks like a breach of faith rather than an ordinary exercise of judgment.

No regulator will ordinarily call you to account for that silence, and a friendship has no standard form and a household decision has no prescribed disclosure date. Without a rule, the pressure remains real and leaves you alone with the question of whether the fact should be said before it becomes expensive to hear. Pressure can grow quietly because the person who knows the inconvenient fact also knows the comforts of silence: the conversation remains smooth, the plan remains intact, and no immediate conflict has to be faced. Yet a silence that preserves comfort for the speaker can move cost onto the person who needed a chance to decide, which is why professional duties focus not simply on whether a statement was eventually made but on whether it was made while its recipient could still use it. Perfect foresight is not the demand. The demand is to prevent knowledge from being used as a private privilege when it has become part of another person's choice.

This is one reason regulated work can be a relief, and the professional need not consult mood, optimism, or the immediate prospect of a transaction. Its standard supplies a reason that does not depend on winning the argument. It makes candour less heroic and more routine. People do not reliably become frank at the instant frankness becomes costly.

A person can resent the form that interrupts an easy conversation. You can also rely on it. Such a form assumes that an interested professional may be reluctant at exactly the wrong moment. It arranges the work around that ordinary weakness. It asks what was known, when it was known, and whether the person who needed it had it while a real choice remained.

That inquiry is not a licence for theatre, and a page can be handed over, signed, and placed in a file while the recipient remains hurried or confused. Delivery is not communication, and the professional still has to treat the form as an occasion to make the relevant matter intelligible rather than as evidence that responsibility has shifted to the other person. There is a further ordinary-life version of this problem. Imagine a person paying for a course of study that no longer fits their life. Once suitable, the syllabus made sense, and the student bought materials, rearranged evenings, and told people why the qualification mattered. Gradually the work no longer leads where expected, or the student continues chiefly because stopping would force an admission about the cost already spent. No institution may be hiding anything. In this case, the missing disclosure may be internal. The original reason has weakened, but saying so is postponed because the sentence would make the next decision unavoidable. Attendance continues as notes accumulate, while another section is made to carry the hope of changing the student's view. The student is not without information. Instead, the moment at which information becomes a conclusion is being avoided. More effort already invested makes it easier to treat delay as patience rather than as a choice to preserve a story.

Often the useful fact is the one that interrupts momentum. Licensed work makes that interruption explicit, and a real-estate licensee cannot improve a material fact because it is inconvenient. A mortgage professional cannot make a difficult term harmless by placing it late in the process, and the question is not whether disclosure will preserve ease. It is whether another person needs the fact before deciding.

I learned a related discipline in law. A client might have a strong position, a sympathetic account, or a confident manner. None of that relieved counsel of confronting authority that cut the other way, and that work was not personal modesty. It was part of the job. The work of a lawyer differs from real-estate and mortgage work, yet each setting gives an informational advantage a defined consequence.

In all three settings, the rule does not make the final choice for anyone, and a buyer may proceed. A borrower may accept the loan, and a client may maintain a position despite adverse authority. Disclosure does not abolish risk, disagreement, or regret. It places the burden of choice with the person who will live with its consequence.

That is the external side of the matter, and my own trading had no comparable machinery. I had information in abundance: prices moved, screens updated, and tools surfaced activity quickly. An intraday trade is a purchase and sale within the same market day, often made in the hope of profiting from a short movement. Scalping is an especially rapid form of such trading, seeking small moves repeatedly. A position is the investment you still hold. Closing a position means ending that exposure by selling or buying back what you opened.

The terms are simple enough, and their practical force is not. When a position moved against me, I could see the adverse fact without giving it a status that required action. I could call it temporary. I could wait for another display. I could take the next movement as a reason to postpone the sentence that mattered: my reason for holding this position has failed.

An unrealised loss is especially easy to mishandle. It is a loss already shown by the current value of something you still hold, even though you have not yet closed the position and made the loss final in the account. Money has already been exposed to the loss, and leaving the position open does not make the difference unreal. It only postpones the act of acknowledging it.

No other person's property decision was entrusted to me in that account, and the comparison has limits. A market loss is not a concealed property fact and it is not a loan term a borrower needed to receive. Still, the absence of an external recipient did not make the facts immaterial to the person whose money was at stake. It removed the social friction that might have made evasion harder.

In licensed work, a fact has a path. It moves from the professional's knowledge into the other person's decision before that decision closes around it. In my account, an adverse fact could remain a passing observation before becoming an old one. It could then disappear beneath the next session. No required record preserved why I entered, why I stayed, or what had changed.

That absence matters more than a failure of filing, and better records might have helped, though a record is useful only if it must answer a question someone is prepared to ask. In regulated work, the questions arrive from outside. What did you know? When did you know it? What did you tell the person who needed to know? My private account allowed the first two questions to fade before the third was ever put.

You may recognise that freedom in a smaller part of your own life, and a subscription you no longer use can remain active because cancelling it would require a moment of honest attention. A medical appointment can be postponed because the result might demand a decision. A disagreement can continue because neither person wants to state the fact that would change the terms of the relationship. In each case, information may already be present. The difficulty is not discovery. It is granting the fact its consequence while something useful can still be done.

This is why self-regard is such a poor regulator. It has no shortage of flattering names for delay. It can call concealment tact, call refusal to decide prudence, and call a wish for more time open-mindedness. Those words are not always false. They become dangerous when nobody requires you to say what you have withheld, from whom, and for how long.

A professional rule does not solve the problem of judgment. It cannot make a buyer choose wisely or a borrower calculate calmly. It cannot supply a fact nobody knows. Its value lies elsewhere. It makes it harder for the person with information to treat another person's ignorance as a convenience.

My two licences have made the contrast plain, and in one part of my working life, candour is a condition of being trusted with an informational advantage. In the other, I let inconvenient information remain private until privacy became a way of giving it no place at all. The screen continued to show what it showed. I continued to decide whether the fact counted yet.

The same question can be carried into any unregulated decision. You need not create a tribunal for every hesitation. You can ask instead whether someone affected by your choice would need this fact before deciding, then ask whether you are using timing to keep the choice easy for yourself. Materiality is a useful word because it resists two opposite mistakes, and one mistake is treating every faint concern as if it must halt the work. The other is treating the fact that actually bears on a choice as merely another detail among many. A professional has to distinguish those errors without using the need for judgment as permission to avoid judgment. The question is practical. Would this fact reasonably matter to the person deciding whether to proceed, and does that person have it before the practical room for choice begins to close?

That question is not answered by the professional's hope that the issue will turn out well, and hope can be decent and necessary in ordinary life. It is a poor substitute for disclosure where another person must bear the result. You may believe that an uncertain difficulty will not become serious. You may even be right. The relevant point is that your confidence does not entitle you to make the other person's decision inside a version of events from which the difficulty has been removed.

Consider the ordinary irritation of a car that has begun making an unfamiliar noise. A driver may turn the radio up for a week because the sound is intermittent and an appointment will take time. The car still starts, the sound has not returned today, or a repair might cost more than can comfortably be faced. Each statement may be true. None answers the practical question of whether a small fact has been allowed to become a larger problem by being withheld from oneself. A mechanic cannot diagnose a noise never described. More importantly, no responsible plan can be made around a condition deliberately left unnamed. The useful act is not panic. It is the plain sentence that permits a decision: something has changed. I need to know what it means before I continue to rely on the old assumption.

That small scene is not a moral allegory about cars. It shows why timing has weight. When the noise first appears, you may have many options. You can listen, arrange an inspection, alter a journey, or decide that the evidence does not yet justify more action. After the car fails at an inconvenient moment, many of those options have narrowed. The later fact is still a fact. It has simply arrived after delay has done part of the deciding for you.

This also applies when disclosure is supplied as paperwork, and a person can receive a document at the correct stage and still be pushed through it as though the signature were the whole purpose. That is not enough. The form fixes the subject and the moment, which are important achievements, but it cannot do the thinking for the recipient. A conscientious professional gives the matter enough shape that the person can recognise what is being decided. The professional does not have to remove uncertainty. He has to refrain from using another person's uncertainty as a quiet source of advantage.

There is no sentimental claim in that requirement, and transactions can remain difficult after the relevant facts are stated. A buyer may decide that a property remains worthwhile. A borrower may conclude that the terms fit the need. The person may simply disagree with the professional's view of the risk. Candour does not require a professional to secure the outcome he would prefer for the other person. It requires him to leave the other person with the information needed to own the outcome.

This becomes more exacting when people have already invested attention, and an offer can gather emotional force before it gathers legal force. A proposed move can reorganise a family's imagination before anyone signs. A loan can begin to feel settled because other arrangements have been made around it. That is why a late disclosure may be accurate in language while inadequate in use. It reaches a person after momentum has acquired its own argument.

Versions of that pressure appear outside any licensed field. Suppose a person has agreed to host others for an important gathering, then discovers that the cost will be substantially more than expected. One response is to keep the fact private while looking for a solution. Another is to promise that the others will be told if the numbers become impossible. Meanwhile, they make travel plans and decline alternatives because they believe the arrangement is secure. The generous impulse to spare them worry can quietly become control over information they would have used differently. By the time the host speaks, their freedom may be technically intact and practically thin. They can still change course, but the cost of changing has become part of a choice made on their behalf.

Private life will sometimes require discretion, and not every thought should be delivered at the first moment it occurs. The discipline is not indiscriminate confession. It is recognising the difference between a passing concern that needs time and a fact whose useful time is being consumed by your silence. You can make that distinction without pretending to be certain. You can say what you know, say what you do not know, and refuse to let uncertainty become a reason for another person to be kept in the dark.

My own mistake in trading was not that I lacked facts, and the screens supplied facts continuously. Nor was it that every change in price demanded a response. Judgment would be impossible on that basis.

My failure was more private. I had no settled way to separate a fact that called for another look from a fact that called for concession. I had no record that could prevent the distinction from changing whenever continuation became more comfortable than an end.

An outside standard has a particular advantage over a private intention. It gives the adverse fact a recipient. Once you must tell another person what has changed, you have to give the change words. You have to identify the point rather than letting it remain a vague discomfort. That discipline will not make anyone wise. It does make it harder to preserve a preferred conclusion by keeping the counterevidence unformed.

A person can build a modest version of that discipline without pretending that every private decision is professional work. You can write down the fact that would alter your decision. You can name the date on which you will revisit it. You can tell the person affected before their alternatives disappear. The point is not to create more paperwork. It is to give inconvenient information a place outside the part of you that benefits from calling it premature.

A rule about material facts has value partly because it does not wait for a professional to feel certain that the fact will ruin the transaction. Certainty may come too late. A person deciding about a property needs the relevant fact while uncertainty can still be weighed, not after someone else has privately decided that the risk is probably acceptable. This is a demanding form of restraint. It asks the person with more experience to distinguish between a fact that needs to be raised and a fear that has merely occurred. It also prevents experience from becoming a private licence to decide that an inexperienced person would be better off not knowing. You can see why the rule needs judgment. A long catalogue of remote possibilities can obscure a decision as effectively as silence. The task is to identify the information whose absence would deform the choice, then to put it where the person making the choice can use it.

There is a reason that task cannot be reduced to a ritual. A disclosure can be complete in form yet evasive in spirit if it is offered in a way that makes understanding unlikely. Equally, a professional can use warmth and apparent helpfulness to avoid the one point that needs a plain answer. Neither failure is cured by calling the conversation cooperative. You may leave an interaction feeling that everyone was pleasant. The relevant question is whether the person with less information was able to see the term, the relationship, or the property fact that should have affected the decision. Rules have a procedural shape because procedure creates a trace. Their real point is practical: the person at risk of making a costly choice should not have to discover the central difficulty only after the professional has secured the easier outcome.

Ordinary life offers a less formal version when a group is planning an expense together. Suppose one person is the first to learn that a proposed arrangement will cost more than everyone expects. There may be a sound reason to wait briefly while the figures are checked. There may also be a strong reason to wait because stating the number will disappoint people who are already enthusiastic. The distinction between those reasons matters. If the wait lasts only long enough to make the information accurate, the group is being helped to decide. If it lasts until deposits are paid or alternatives have disappeared, the same number becomes a confession that arrives after the group has been carried forward by silence. No legal form is needed to understand the difference. It appears in the moment when the fact moves from useful news to an obstacle everyone else must now absorb.

That difference also explains why a record can help without becoming a cure. Writing down what was known at a particular moment does not make a person candid. Someone can write defensively, select what looks favourable, or return to the page later with a story that flatters the earlier choice. Yet a record has one modest advantage over memory. It fixes a statement before the next movement supplies an incentive to edit the meaning of the last one. The record may never need to be shown to anyone. It can still expose the gap between the reason given before acting and the reason later preferred in memory. In a private decision, that gap is often the only available counterpart to the professional question: what was known, and what was done because it was known?

This is not an argument for making every personal decision public. Some judgments are properly private. Some concerns need time before they are fit to state.

The point is narrower and more useful. When your silence changes another person's practical options, or when it preserves your own preferred story against facts you have already seen, silence has ceased to be neutral. The relevant discipline is not self-punishment. It is a willingness to give the adverse fact enough definition that it can interrupt you before momentum decides in its place.

The licensed setting makes the value of interruption unusually visible. A property decision or a loan can gather force through small steps that nobody experiences as final until the alternatives have narrowed. A clear disclosure does not stop the process merely to demonstrate caution. It puts a moment of recognition into the process while recognition can still alter what happens next. In private life, that moment has to be created. A person can pause before another payment, say that a plan depends on a fact not yet resolved, or state that the original reason no longer carries its former weight. None of these acts guarantees a good outcome. Each makes it harder to drift into an outcome that was never examined.

Private freedom is valuable, but it offers no protection against selective attention. It leaves you free to retain information, delay a conclusion, and call the delay reasonable. A professional obligation cannot be carried whole into every ordinary choice. Its underlying question can. What fact would change the decision if it were stated plainly now? Once you have asked that question, you may still decide to proceed. You will at least know that proceeding is a decision rather than a continuation protected by silence.

Disclosure has force not because it treats every difficult fact as decisive. A disclosed fact may be serious, manageable, uncertain, or ultimately unimportant. What it cannot be is privately converted into irrelevance by the person who benefits from its omission. This is the practical dignity of the person receiving the information: not a promise that every choice will be safe, but a chance to choose without another person silently arranging which risks are visible. The obligation is still to leave the choice recognisably theirs, even when others would have chosen differently. In private life, that standard is often too demanding to be enforced from outside. It remains a good test of whether the timing of silence has become a way of taking control over a decision that belongs partly to someone else, or a way of avoiding the decision that belongs to the silent person. No licensing rule is needed to see the value of that test. It needs enough honesty to notice when a fact is being held back because its arrival would end the comfort of carrying on as though nothing had changed. When the next useful step is now plain enough to take, the person who will pay for the choice still needs a clear account. State the fact that would change the decision while there is still time for it to matter.

## CHAPTER SIX

# Two Hundred and Ninety-Three Dollars and Fifty Cents a Month

Those screens made a convincing office. This is not a complaint about them. An office has surfaces for receiving information, instruments for sorting it, plus tasks that can be performed with evident seriousness, and mine held Finviz, Trade Ideas, TradingView, plus thinkorswim. They gave my mornings the visible structure of prepared work.

Finviz cost $39.50 a month, and Trade Ideas cost $254 a month. Together they cost $293.50 a month, and across those seventeen months, that came to roughly $4,990. During that period, my losses from intraday scalping of various stocks exceeded $20,000. Here, the arithmetic belongs in plain sight, and the subscriptions were not hidden purchases or foolish toys. They were capable tools for the work they claimed to do, and Finviz narrows thousands of companies to those matching conditions a user has chosen. Trade Ideas watches the market continuously and brings a developing condition forward. TradingView makes price movement readable on a chart. thinkorswim is the execution platform, the place where observation can become an order.

A person new to trading may hear those names as a single blur of technology. They are different rooms in the same office. A screener begins with a large market and returns a shorter list of companies that fit stated conditions. A scanner keeps watching after the list has been made, looking for activity as it occurs. Charts turn changing prices into pictures across chosen stretches of time. An execution platform accepts the instruction to buy or sell.

Each function is useful, and none is judgment. Finviz was where a broad field became manageable, and a ticker is the short label by which a company's shares are identified on a trading screen. A screener can return a table of tickers, each accompanied by information chosen for the search, and the user may then move from a field too large to watch to a smaller group that appears to deserve attention. That reduction is valuable. It does not tell you why a particular company deserves action, how much risk you should accept, or when a promising item has ceased to be promising.

At the beginning of an hour, the result can feel orderly. A list appears, and rows can be sorted while a watchlist, which is simply a saved collection of symbols you want to follow, gathers candidates in one place. Volume means the number of shares changing hands over a period. Volatility means how sharply prices are moving. Both can help show that something is active. Neither tells you what that activity means for your own decision.

Nothing on the screen asks what you plan to do with the list. Trade Ideas made the next stage feel more immediate, and a real-time scanner looks for conditions while the market is open rather than waiting for you to search manually. When an alert fires, it brings a symbol or condition to attention at the moment the programme has found what it was set to notice. Its arrival can be brisk: a name, a movement, a reason to look. It does not arrive as a command. It is an invitation to inspect.

That distinction is easy to lose when you are sitting at the desk. You have paid for a service that sees faster than a person can see by moving from page to page. The alert confirms that the machinery is working. You look at the name before opening a chart. The next step is close enough that attention begins to resemble a conclusion. Yet the alert has answered a limited question. It has shown that a stated condition appeared. It has not told you whether the condition matters, whether it fits a plan, or whether you are looking for evidence to support a decision you have already begun to prefer.

A chart did something different, and TradingView displayed price movement in a form the eye can absorb quickly, over a time span the user selected. It could make a rise, a fall, or a period of hesitation visible, and a chart pattern is a recurring shape traders believe may be relevant to what prices do next. Such a pattern may give the eye a language for comparison. It cannot tell you whether the pattern will hold, what other people intend, or how much of your own hope has entered the reading.

Because a chart is persuasive, its limits matter. It replaces a mass of changing figures with a coherent line of movement. Such a display can be enlarged or reduced, and one period can be compared with another. Still, it will faithfully show the path prices have taken. It cannot show the reason you formed for acting, the point at which that reason failed, or the personal cost of refusing to let it fail.

A spread is the small gap between the price available to a buyer and the price available to a seller at a given moment, and that gap is part of what a trader faces when entering or leaving. It is a fact on a screen. It does not decide whether the trader should enter at all. thinkorswim brought the work closest to consequence, and an execution platform provides order entry: the means to send an instruction to buy or sell. A position is the investment still held after an order has been made, and closing a position ends that exposure by selling or buying back what was opened. A stop-loss is an order intended to close a position if the price reaches a stated loss point. These are real controls. They put structure near the moment of action. They still depend on a user who has decided what structure is needed and is willing to honour it.

This is where paper trading deserves a plain explanation, and paper trading is simulated trading:

the platform records an imaginary purchase or sale as though it were real, without the user putting actual money at risk. It can be a useful way to learn how orders work or to test whether a method can be followed. It can also mislead because the user knows, however seriously he tries to practise, that an imagined loss does not require the same concession as an actual loss involving money that matters to the person at risk. Each click may be the same. Actual money is not. A person who appears disciplined with a simulation may discover a different self when the decision has a real cost.

Backtesting has a related limit. It means applying a proposed method to past market data to see how it would have behaved. This exercise can expose a weak idea before real money is involved, yet it cannot show how you will react when the result is current but ambiguous and personally unwelcome. Past data supplies examples. It does not supply a future willingness to concede.

An unrealised loss reveals the difference with particular force. It is the loss shown by the current value of a position you have not yet closed. A loss has already affected what the holding is worth, and keeping the position open does not erase it. It leaves the account exposed while allowing the person watching to postpone the final act of agreement.

I do not say any of this to blame the tools. They performed their stated functions. They reduced a vast field of activity into information that could be watched, sorted, and acted upon more quickly, and a scanner could identify movement that might otherwise pass unnoticed. A chart could display a change in a form the eye absorbs rapidly. An execution platform could place the person watching close to the point at which watching becomes action. Those are considerable achievements.

Their usefulness made the problem more respectable, and had the equipment been plainly useless, buying it would have been easy to dismiss as vanity. It offered a real advantage in finding activity, comparing what had been found, and keeping the work in view, and the danger was treating that advantage as an answer to another question. Better information does not decide which apparent signal deserves weight. It does not decide which loss requires an end. It does not decide which prior rule should take precedence when a screen supplies fresh reasons to keep looking.

My routine had the rhythm of work. I looked for activity. I narrowed what I was seeing. I opened charts. Next, I watched movement. The platform remained near at hand. Each action led naturally to the next, and the sequence converted an undefined field into manageable tasks. Nothing in that routine felt like avoidance at first.

That was precisely its attraction, and avoidance commonly looks idle from the outside, like a person declining to make a call or open a letter. At the desk it looked industrious, and there were lists to compare and alerts to consider. I could move from one to the next with the clean sensation of progress. I could postpone a decision while remaining busy enough not to feel that I had postponed it.

Preparation contains real work. You should not mistake this argument for praise of ignorance or impatience. A person who refuses to prepare is not displaying admirable decisiveness, and markets move quickly. Information is uneven. An unaided glance tells you little about what you have missed. A person acting intraday has good reason to want tools that scan, display, and organise.

The trouble begins after the reasonable purchase, and a screen full of active information can tell you that you have more to inspect. It cannot tell you that inspection is now serving as a refuge from a conclusion, and no amount of added information can supply the rule for surrendering a view you have begun to defend. That rule has to exist somewhere other than the display. Suppose a person pays for a fitness service that records sleep, meals, exercise and weight. It may be excellent. The record can show patterns that a tired person would otherwise miss. A graph may make it obvious that weekends undo the routine built during the week. Reminders may arrive at useful times. One month can be compared with another, and the exactness of the apparatus can make attention feel more serious. Yet the service cannot decide whether the habit it has made visible will change. It cannot choose dinner, bedtime, or the conversation in which a person admits that a routine does not fit the life actually being led. An hour may be spent studying reports because studying them feels responsible. The useful work may be the shorter and less flattering act of changing one part of the day. Information has done its part. Judgment begins where the record stops.

That pattern does not make the service a bad purchase. It makes the purchase incomplete. A person can have excellent measurements and still decline to give their adverse implication a consequence, and the more detailed the record becomes, the easier it may be to select the encouraging part while postponing the part that asks for change. A person can also become very skilled at reporting the record without ever submitting to it. Someone may know the average, trend, exception, and technical explanation for every disappointing week, yet continue to treat the report as a substitute for the awkward choice it has made plain. Such a system rewards attention because attention is visible: numbers arrive, boxes are completed, and a history accumulates that can be discussed with impressive precision. Judgment is quieter. It appears when a person decides that the pattern calls for a change in behaviour rather than a more elegant account of why it occurred.

No application can make that turn on someone else's behalf, because the turn belongs to values and priorities that are not in the data. A demanding regimen may reasonably be judged not worth its cost. It may also be judged worth it. More importantly, the decision becomes visible once the apparatus is no longer asked to relieve its user of having one. At that stage, another dashboard can provide more detail. It cannot provide the courage to accept the implication of the detail already supplied. A person may have enough evidence to know that the current arrangement is not working, while still needing to decide whether change is worth the inconvenience it will cause. That is not a failure of the service. It is the point at which a record stops being a record and becomes a demand for a person to decide what matters more.

Consider a different ordinary system: a household subscription that brings constant news, comparisons, reviews and recommendations. It can be genuinely helpful when a person is deciding what to buy, how to travel or whom to hire. Tabs can be opened, articles saved and prices compared while the person tells themselves that one more source will reduce the chance of regret. At some point, the information has already supplied enough to make a choice. By then, the reason for remaining in research may have changed. The person may be avoiding the risk of choosing, the possibility of disappointment, or the admission that no option will be perfect. Meanwhile, the apparatus continues to provide fresh material, so there is no need to sit with the fact that more material is no longer the missing ingredient. The subscription is not holding anyone there. Its use may be.

Most readers have some equivalent. It may be a course, a budgeting system, a calendar application, a stream of professional advice, or unread material bought in the name of becoming more prepared. The thing is often good at what it does, and the harder question is whether you are buying help with a decision or buying a respectful way to defer it. A decision rule is less visible than a screen. It may be a sentence written before pressure begins, a maximum loss accepted in advance, or a condition that ends a view when it occurs. I did not give myself a record of rules that could be compared with what I actually did, and that absence limits any confident account of the precise moments at which I failed to stop. It does not alter the fact that the applications could not write the missing rule for me.

A person with a clear method may use a scanner well, and a screener can serve a defined task. A chart can test a view against an unwelcome possibility, and a stop-loss can make a stated limit operational. The fair conclusion is not that anyone should throw the tools away. It is that a tool supports candour only when its user has made room for candour.

The machinery offered no external questioner. It did not know why I had entered a position, what use the money served in my life, or the point at which persistence had ceased to be rational. I would not want a machine to pretend that it knew those things, yet the absence of an outside questioner made the visible activity even more seductive. There was always another filter to adjust, another chart to enlarge, another movement to watch, another item of information to compare.

A serious person likes tools that can be inspected, with prices, features, settings and visible outputs. A subscription can be identified by its intended service, and one display can be compared with another to explain why the second seems clearer. These things feel accountable because they are concrete. A personal rule has no such display case. It may be only a line written before the market opens: if this condition occurs, I close the position. Such a line can be wrong. It can be rigid. It can require revision. Its value is that it gives the later self something to answer, rather than allowing every new fact to be absorbed into a new explanation.

In retrospect, the difference became clearer: I had paid for access to better information and received it. What I had granted myself was permission to treat possession of information as evidence that I had met a more demanding obligation, and that distinction separates the service provided from the story I built around using it. The same shift can be heard in a person's language. Instead of saying there is a rule, the person begins to say there is more information. Instead of asking whether a condition has occurred, the person asks what the next display suggests. The first language creates a place where an answer may close the matter. The second has no natural stopping point.

No stopping point can feel like freedom. It leaves a person able to revise as facts arrive. Revision is often sensible, and a rigid response to changing circumstances can become another form of denial. Flexibility without a declared boundary, though, is often only a courteous name for doing nothing after the boundary has been crossed.

No application concealed that limit, and a scanner calls itself a scanner. A chart shows the chart before it, while a platform offers means for watching and acting. None promised restraint, an accurate account of your motives, or protection from a conclusion you did not want. The promises I heard beyond that were largely my own.

At the end of a session, the applications could remain open without asking anything of me, and their columns kept changing. Their charts kept drawing, and the desk looked occupied, alert, and ready for a better decision. It did not know that the decision already required was the one I had not made. The hour-by-hour experience matters because the sequence is so persuasive, and a user might begin with Finviz before the market opens, reduce a broad field to a manageable list, then keep a few names in a watchlist while the day begins. The list does not feel like a mere list. It feels like the result of a selection process. Time has been spent identifying conditions, and the field has been narrowed. The remaining names have acquired an appearance of earned attention, even though the screening process has established only that they meet the conditions chosen for the screen.

As the market moves, Trade Ideas can make that attention feel urgent, and a scanner is valuable because a person cannot hold the whole market in view unaided. An alert supplies a reason to look now rather than later. It may direct the eye to a change that has happened quickly. An alert is an event in the working day. It creates a small pulse of relevance. Nothing in its arrival establishes that the user should buy, sell, or even continue watching after the first inspection.

A chart then gives the movement a narrative shape, and the user can change the time horizon, compare the present with what came before, and look for a pattern that seems familiar. That work can be thoughtful. It can also be a place where the mind starts turning a visible movement into a private prediction. A chart can show that a price rose after a point, fell through a point, or moved within a range. It cannot show whether the reason you are giving the movement is a tested premise or an explanation invented after you wanted to act.

Order entry makes the final transition unnervingly small, and a symbol has already been found. An alert has already made it current, and a chart has already made it legible. By the time an order is available, the act can feel like the natural completion of work already done. Yet the order is not the completion of research in the way a sentence completes a paragraph. It is a new decision that exposes money. Smoothness in the route to that decision is a feature when the reasoning is sound. It is a danger when smoothness hides the need for a separate pause.

A later hour can repeat the same sequence with a different emotional colour, and a position that has moved favourably may make continued attention feel justified. A position that has moved adversely may make the chart seem full of reasons to wait, and the scanner can offer a fresh possibility elsewhere. The platform remains ready. The screen never becomes blank enough to force an accounting. Every tool is doing its work. The person still has to decide whether the work is serving a plan or protecting a reluctance to end one.

That is why good interfaces can be psychologically powerful without being at fault. They remove friction from tasks that users reasonably want to perform. A well-made screener saves time. An effective alert reduces delay. A clear chart makes comparison easier. Professional-grade order entry avoids needless obstacles at the moment a person has decided to act. Those benefits are real. They also mean that the user needs a source of restraint which does not depend on the interface becoming less helpful.

Think of the same distinction in a kitchen full of excellent appliances. In that kitchen, a precise scale can measure ingredients. A timer can keep track of time. A recipe service can offer substitutions when something is missing. Each tool can improve the chance that dinner turns out well. None can decide whether a cook is preparing food for the people who will eat, whether enough has been bought for everyone, or whether a complicated recipe is being used to avoid admitting that a simpler meal would serve the evening better. A person may become absorbed in settings, measurements and options because those are concrete tasks with clear answers. Judgment about what the occasion actually requires remains with the cook. Better equipment makes the work easier. It does not exempt anyone from deciding what work is worth doing.

Trading screens carried the same kind of authority. They made visible facts that should not have been ignored. They were much better than ignorance. Still, no display could make the next inference for me. It could not determine whether a price movement defeated my reason for acting. It could not decide whether a stop-loss should exist, where it should sit, or whether I would honour it when the moment came.

Information gives a person material for judgment. It does not manufacture the willingness to use judgment against a desired result.

This is not a minor distinction between theory and practice. It is the place where a person can remain intensely busy while leaving the most consequential decision unmade. As the apparatus becomes more competent, the busyness can look more credible. You can be reading, sorting, measuring, or responding to alerts. From the outside, and often from the inside, that looks like care. It becomes avoidance only when the activity is no longer helping you decide and is instead helping you avoid the cost of deciding.

A private rule does not have to be grand. It can be a note before the day begins that says what would invalidate a view, what amount of loss will end participation, or what evidence will require a pause. Any rule may need revision. It may be poorly designed. Those are questions worth facing. A rule that can be criticised is still more useful than a preference that can change shape whenever it is challenged.

You may have an equivalent apparatus nowhere near a market. It may be a recurring subscription that supplies endless expert commentary, an application that turns life into notifications, or a system at work that promises a clearer picture if you only keep feeding it inputs. Such systems often repay the money spent on them. A warning is not an instruction to abandon a useful source of information. It is to notice the instant at which gathering one more piece of information becomes a respectable way to avoid the conclusion already supported by the pieces you have.

These tools were excellent at what they claimed; Finviz could reduce the field. Trade Ideas could surface activity quickly. TradingView could make price action visible. thinkorswim could place execution close at hand and offer paper trading for practise without real money at risk. Their excellence made them worth paying for. Their limits made them unable to do the one part of the work that was mine.

The screen also changes the scale at which attention is experienced. Without a scanner, a person can feel the limits of individual attention more readily. With a scanner, a large field is reduced into manageable signals and the day begins to feel knowable. That is a genuine benefit. It can also encourage a quiet overstatement of what has been achieved. The machine has made the field easier to survey. It has not converted a survey into a reason for risking money. You still have to decide whether the condition you saw has meaning in relation to your plan, whether the plan had a sound basis, and whether the price of being wrong is one you are prepared to bear.

A good chart can create a similar overstatement because it gives a restless sequence of prices a visual order. It permits comparison without pretending that every movement has the same weight. Used well, that is a disciplined improvement over guessing from a single number. Used defensively, the same clarity can help a person keep revisiting the part of the picture that permits hope. You can enlarge the period that makes a decline look less serious. You can narrow the period that makes a rise look decisive. The chart has not deceived you. It has supplied several true views of the same movement. Judgment lies in deciding which view actually bears on the reason you had for acting.

An alert creates another form of pressure. It arrives at a time when speed appears to have value. It often does. The user can feel that the opportunity is perishable because the message itself is current. This is where a rule has to be ready before the notice appears. Once the alert has placed a name in front of you, the mind is already beginning to treat attention as a claim on action. A prior rule can ask a simple question: does this fit the kind of decision I intended to make? It does not have to eliminate speed. It prevents speed from deciding which standards survive the moment.

There is an ordinary counterpart whenever a service turns current information into a sequence of prompts. An email system can show a full inbox, a project board can show newly urgent tasks, and a news service can show a stream that never quite ends. Each prompt may describe something real. Still, a day spent responding to every fresh signal can leave the work that actually matters untouched. You need some principle for deciding which information changes the plan and which information merely competes for the feeling of being active. The principle may be imperfect. It is better than allowing the apparatus to turn every visible item into a claim on your attention.

That is why I do not regard the $293.50 a month as an indictment of the applications. The tools supplied what the subscriptions promised: speed, organisation, visibility, and an easier route from broad activity to a possible action. The cost is relevant because it made the office feel serious and because the arithmetic belongs with the losses in the same account. It does not prove that the tools caused the losses. A useful instrument can be bought for a reasonable purpose, then used inside a pattern of avoidance. The distinction is essential. Blaming the instrument would be another way of avoiding the decision that only its user could make.

The healthiest use of a tool may therefore begin with a limitation stated in advance. A screener can help you find. An alert can help you notice. A chart can help you compare. An execution platform can help you act. None of those statements describes what you should believe about a particular movement or what consequence you should accept when your belief proves unsound. Once the boundaries are clear, the tools can be treated with respect rather than superstition. You can use their speed without mistaking speed for wisdom. You can value their information without making information a substitute for the decision that information was meant to inform. The purpose of the apparatus is not to make the user feel permanently prepared, nor to make another look feel like a settled reason to keep acting. Its purpose is to make relevant facts easier to see before the user decides what those facts require. That distinction also preserves a fair view of the people who build the tools: they can make better information available without accepting responsibility for judgments that belong to the person who chooses to act. A clear limit does not diminish the service. It prevents the user from turning a useful service into an excuse for postponing the responsibility that no service can assume, especially under the pressure of a live position, when visible activity can make a conclusion already supported by the facts seem hasty, impersonal or needlessly final. Keep the tools that give you useful information, but give the information a rule that can require you to act against your preference.

## CHAPTER SEVEN

# The Feeling of Progress

A clean list can make a difficult matter seem manageable because it gives distinct names to things that had been loose in the mind. It creates edges around a subject that has been leaking into the day, while promising that the parts can now be found again. That promise is often worth keeping. A list can prevent a missed appointment, preserve a useful observation, or expose a difference that a hurried glance would miss. Order is not the enemy of judgment. It is often judgment's necessary assistant.

There is a familiar feeling when a crowded desk becomes labelled piles, an inbox loses its red numbers, or a calendar receives its proper colours. For an hour, the subject feels less threatening because it has been made visible, and visibility produces a small but genuine relief. Hands have done something. A screen has changed. What matters is whether conduct has changed too.

I felt that relief at a screen when I made watchlists, which are lists of stocks a trader has chosen to follow rather than trying to follow the whole market. I made categories, added notes, then refined the categories whenever a new distinction occurred to me, which could happen repeatedly on a single evening. Finviz and Trade Ideas helped sort a large field, while TradingView and thinkorswim offered further ways to see it. These were capable tools that did what they claimed. They could show me information. They could not determine what I would do when information became inconvenient.

A decision has a clear end even if it proves mistaken: a person accepts the invitation or declines it, authorises the repair or stops it, applies for the job or decides not to. Organisation has no comparable border. A folder can always be made more exact, a calendar can take another colour, and a list can acquire another subheading that makes the former arrangement look premature. That openness gives organisation a peculiar power as an avoidance device, since it can continue indefinitely without announcing itself as delay and nobody can demonstrate that the next refinement was unnecessary. Work still looks like work, the organiser still receives the relief of making something orderly, and the cost remains hidden in the question that goes untouched.

This is why an organised person can be less ready to act than a disorganised one. An unorganised person may see the choice plainly because there is nothing left to arrange around it, while an organiser has created an outer task with its own demands that can absorb hours without ever requiring a position. Greater conscientiousness makes the substitute more convincing because careful people are accustomed to believing that further care is an answer. Sometimes it is, while sometimes it merely avoids finding out whether earlier care was enough.

Suppose you have been avoiding an answer to a difficult email involving a relative, a colleague, or an invitation you do not want to accept. You decide to prepare first. You search old threads, put them in date order, then flag sentences that may matter. An opening is drafted until it sounds both kind and guarded. Each small act feels responsible because you have gathered context, recalled the history, and given the matter visible attention. Yet the task was to decide what you will say, and a fuller folder does not alter the relationship while your reply remains unsent. If the organisation gives you another pleasant hour without bringing you nearer to an answer, it may be protecting you from the part that costs something.

That does not make the folder foolish. It may be what lets you reply with care. Its value depends on whether it changes the reply rather than merely postponing it. That distinction is small. Its consequence is not.

Consider someone who is planning a move because the current home has become too costly, too cramped, or simply wrong. She begins with a notebook, then builds tabs for neighbourhoods and costs. Other pages hold photographs, walking times, and notes on the light in each bedroom. All of it is sensible material. A new version follows when the first one looks crowded, while a Saturday disappears into comparing floor plans that she had already rejected. This is not laziness. It may be intelligent work, yet it needs a stopping point if it is to become preparation rather than an occupation. At some point, she has enough to choose a place, renew the lease, or decide that moving is not possible now.

That notebook feels easier because it leaves every door open. Judgment begins when she permits a fact to close one. Such a division appears when a reading list grows faster than it shrinks. Research can become a way to stay adjacent to a choice without entering it. Another article always offers another postponement.

My own system had this quality during intraday trading, which means buying and selling on the same day rather than carrying the stock past the market's close. A note led to another note, a category divided into smaller categories, and a lively screen made the work feel current even when it did not alter my next act. I treated the growing system as proof that I was taking the activity seriously, though I was often improving the appearance of preparation rather than deciding with greater care. One question was much plainer: what would this material require me to do differently? I rarely made myself answer it before the pressure began.

My key distinction was between material that described the market and a rule that governed me. A list could tell me which stocks had moved, but it could not tell me whether movement justified exposure, how much loss I was prepared to accept, or when a promising idea had become a reason to step away. The first kind of knowledge is descriptive, while the second is a commitment made before the moment supplies an excuse to abandon it. I liked the first because it made me feel informed without requiring the embarrassment of being tested. A commitment could be wrong. A list of observations could simply be expanded.

That is also why systems tend to grow at the boundary between attention and action. Attention is admirable. It is hard to object to a person who has read more, filed more, or noticed more distinctions. Action introduces a different standard because it must be assessed by what followed. A system that remains on the attentive side of that boundary can borrow the moral credit of action without submitting to its exposure.

Real answers create tests. You have to state what evidence would make you stop, decline, wait, or change course. Then you leave that statement in place when the evidence arrives. A label never faces that risk. Renaming is easy. Moving it is easy. An interesting label can survive forever.

A person managing a household budget can meet the same temptation after an unexpected home repair has already begun. At first, the estimate felt survivable, though the work now costs far more. Before deciding whether to continue, the owner builds a spreadsheet recording the money already spent alongside a separate estimate for the work still required. That file may be excellent because it shows where the money went, yet it cannot decide whether further spending is justified at this moment. If it becomes more impressive each week while nobody asks what limit remains, the record has become a place to store reluctance. Harder still is writing a number at which the work stops, even when that number makes earlier spending painful to admit.

Order becomes evasive when it reports only the past. A useful record reaches forward. It says what a known fact will mean for the next action. The other kind can be called diligence because it looks like diligence. Its polished surface is part of the appeal.

A record becomes useful when it gives the future a claim on the present. The homeowner's spreadsheet might contain a line reading: no further work without a revised estimate, while the job-search file might record: apply to two positions before saving another ten. Neither sentence supplies courage, but each makes it possible to discover later whether courage was supplied. The record then stops being a museum of activity and becomes an instrument for comparing intention with conduct, a comparison often avoided because it can show that preparation was sincere but insufficient.

The alternative is a record that becomes more decorative as the decision becomes more urgent: colours multiply, filters become clever, and earlier versions are replaced before they can be compared with what actually happened. Nothing looks neglected. Yet nothing has acquired the authority to close an option. A system that cannot create a cost for its owner is not yet a system of judgment. It is a display of attention.

For me, the visible object was often a watchlist, which narrowed my attention without telling me what a price movement meant or making restraint more likely. In a position, a trader has bought or sold a stock and is exposed to what happens next, while closing a position ends that exposure by taking the opposite action. Those are decisions. The watchlist came before them, so I let the earlier task borrow the authority of the later one. I had arranged material, then gave myself credit for having acted.

A watchlist also offered the comfort of proximity, allowing me to feel close to the action without stating what that closeness was for. A person can get the same sensation from a running list of houses, courses, recipes, or potential purchases. An object becomes familiar through repeated viewing, and familiarity can be mistaken for readiness. Seeing something every day does not establish that it should be chosen. It may only establish that the system has made it easy to see again.

More important is the omitted contrary entry: an honest watchlist would not merely name what deserved attention. It would record what would disqualify it. A household list can do the same. Beside an item marked "consider," place the condition under which consideration ends. Beside a proposed commitment, write the obligation it will displace. Such entries make the list less agreeable because they introduce refusal. They also restore the list to its proper job: serving a choice rather than simulating one.

You can test a system with one question: what does it prevent? A calendar that never causes you to decline an invitation is decoration, while a budget that never curbs a purchase is an archive. A reading plan that never changes your view is a collection of titles. The test is not whether the system is beautiful. It is whether it interrupts you when interruption costs something.

That authority must be arranged before pressure arrives, because once the answer is pressing a person can usually find a reason to create one more list. The list may be sensible, though it may also be the last pleasant task available before an answer must be given. Before adding a category, a person can say what it will change. Before opening another article, state what answer would permit the reading to stop. Those sentences may show that more information is needed. They may show that you already have enough.

There is another version of this problem in a shared project. A group agrees that a decision is needed. It then makes a board that records every dependency, owner, risk, and possible date. That board may reveal real confusion. It may also let the group avoid saying which risk matters most. Many people have watched this happen when a meeting ends with more categories than it began with, plus a promise to return once everyone has "looked into" the open items. Nobody has lied. Work has occurred. Yet the decision remains safely in the future, protected by the respectable claim that the picture is still incomplete. A project can fail in this manner without anyone appearing idle. It becomes busy around the point at which somebody would have to choose a cost.

Collective manners often conceal the missing decision because nobody wants to be the person who asks for a choice before every uncertainty has been reduced. Nobody wants to sound careless about a risk that is genuinely present. A group can keep honouring each concern until the project has no energy left for the question that created the concerns. In that setting, a useful chair does not demand certainty. A useful chair asks what the group will do if certainty does not arrive, shifting the meeting from inventory to responsibility.

Private life has its own version. A family calendar may accurately show that every weekend is occupied. It does not by itself decide which obligation should be released when exhaustion appears. A schedule can become a highly competent witness to an overfull life. It starts to help only when it makes an event impossible, a boundary visible, or a refusal easier to utter.

Good preparation has a relation to an ending. Material is gathered so that a question can become answerable, a schedule is established so that a commitment can be made, and alternatives are written down so that one can be selected. When preparation has no imagined end, it begins to feed upon itself. More detail creates a need for more detail. A person can then confuse completeness with safety, though complete knowledge is rarely available in the matters that trouble us most. Waiting gives uncertainty a permanent address. That address can be furnished with better labels, better folders, and better intentions while nothing in the room requires anyone to leave it.

Think of someone who suspects that a course of study no longer fits, even though the work may once have been absorbing. The fees, hours, and identity built around the course make reconsideration feel disloyal. Instead of deciding, the person reads programmes and compares credentials, requests testimonials, then saves articles about career paths. Each search postpones the harder sentence: I may need to stop. The delay invites sympathy because the decision carries real loss, while earlier effort cannot be recovered. Friends may have expectations, while a new direction may be uncertain. Still, information about every possible alternative cannot answer whether the present path should continue. Only a judgment about the present path can do that.

A list has another seductive feature: it gives a person a visible measure of effort. You can count pages read, messages tagged, or sources saved. That count may be useful, yet it creates a private scoreboard whose numbers are easier to improve than the underlying situation. A person researching a job change can save fifty positions without applying for one. Someone trying to mend a friendship can draft ten versions of an apology without making the call, while the count becomes a substitute for the result because it offers evidence that the person has not done nothing. The person has not done nothing, while the trouble is that the one act whose result would test the preparation may still have been avoided. A useful note needs a verb. "Monitor this" describes attention, but "cancel if the cost reaches this amount" describes a future act. "Consider alternatives" leaves every route open, whereas "ask for a second estimate before authorising more work" closes one easy escape. The wording matters because your later self will read it under different pressures. A vague note is generous to that later self, while it lets preference choose its own interpretation. A note with a condition is less pleasant, though it makes a claim that can be checked, while it creates the possibility that you will discover you did not follow your own judgment.

In the market, I did not always want that discovery. The screen made review feel like participation, and a new item could arrive before I had asked what the last item had taught me. I could adjust the list after an outcome without admitting that the earlier arrangement had failed to restrain me. A revised system looks forward. It can also erase the evidence that the previous system had no effect, while you can do the same with a personal plan when every bad week produces a new template, a new app, or a newly precise set of goals. Revision is valuable when it responds to evidence, while it becomes evasion when it prevents evidence from accumulating against the person who keeps revising.

A decision also has a date at which it can be reviewed without being quietly undone. The person who chooses a course of study may agree to reassess after a term, rather than treating every difficult week as proof that the course was wrong or every pleasant week as proof that it was right. The point is not to force loyalty to a prior choice. It is to keep a passing mood from using revision as a loophole. A review date creates room for evidence while preventing the question from being reopened every evening.

That discipline is different from stubbornness. Stubbornness refuses evidence because a decision has already been made. Judgment makes a decision answerable to evidence by deciding in advance when the evidence will be considered. The first protects pride. The second protects a person from the pressure of the current hour.

Often, the difference appears in what you choose not to record. A busy organiser may preserve dates, names, costs, and impressions while omitting the prediction that would make the later result meaningful. A person may keep every receipt from a repair without recording the budget at which stopping was intended. Every message in an argument may be retained without a note of what would count as a satisfactory resolution. Such omissions do not have to be deliberate, while they can arise because predictions are embarrassing. They expose what you expected, while a collection of facts is safer because facts can be admired without forcing the collector to say what should follow from them.

An honest system includes a way to disappoint its owner. That is the part I had neglected. If a watchlist made no trade less likely, then it had not yet earned the authority I attributed to it. If a note did not make a later choice harder or easier, it may have preserved an impression without governing conduct. A private system need not be harsh. It only needs to be capable of saying no. A packing list says no to leaving before the passport is found. Your household budget says no to an expense that crowds out rent. One conversation plan says no to raising a grievance when the other person has asked for a different kind of help.

There is a practical mercy in such limits. Without them, every decision must be remade from the beginning while the person is tired, rushed, lonely, or eager for relief. Limits reduce the amount of character required in a bad moment. The decision can be made when more than the immediate reward is visible. Later, when the immediate reward has become loud, the earlier decision can still speak. That is not an attempt to eliminate judgment. It is an attempt to give judgment a longer life than a passing mood. The limit can be revised later if the facts warrant it. What matters is that revision should not occur only when revision is convenient.

A system must be allowed to make its owner uncomfortable. That demanding standard runs against the usual purpose of a private tool: reducing forgotten tasks, producing a sense of command, or making a complicated day appear containable. Those are real benefits. Yet a system that only comforts will be consulted chiefly when it agrees with its owner. A better test comes when it interrupts a preferred plan. Does the budget make a desired purchase harder? Can the calendar make rest defensible? Can a note from last week make today's attractive explanation less believable? If the answer is never yes, the system has not been given enough authority.

This authority need not be rigid. A limit may be changed when circumstances change. A plan may be revised when its premise fails. One condition remains: the change must be named as a change rather than smuggled in as an update to the arrangement. Once that practice is established, a system can hold both flexibility and memory. It can recognise a new fact without pretending that the older fact never made a claim.

I do not mean that every list needs to become a command. Some subjects benefit from open exploration, especially before their terms are clear. A person may need to read widely before deciding what question is being asked. A pile may need sorting before its contents are clear. Order retains its proper value there. Warning begins when the question is already clear but the sorting continues because clarity would require a response. At that point, another evening of organisation may be less like preparation than a way of obtaining the feeling of progress without the exposure of progress itself.

A research phase is particularly hard to end because it can produce genuine discoveries while still avoiding the decision for which the discoveries were gathered. Suppose you are choosing a car after the old one has begun making an unfamiliar noise. You read reliability reports, compare insurance costs, save videos about repairs, and build a table of models that grows more detailed each week. The table may protect you from an expensive mistake. It may also let you postpone the visit to a mechanic or the decision to live without a replacement for now. Your work becomes useful when it clarifies a threshold: this repair is worth approving, this model fits the budget, or this uncertainty is enough to make you wait. Until then, the research can be endless because it is answering questions that do not yet require an answer from you.

Notice how often organisation borrows the language of care. You say you are getting on top of something, staying ahead of it, or making sure nothing slips through. Each phrase describes a real virtue in the right setting. Yet care also includes the willingness to let unwelcome information change the plan. A person who tracks every bill but never looks at the total may be organised without being attentive to the problem. Someone who keeps a perfect family calendar but refuses to discuss the exhaustion it records has created order around an unaddressed fact. Whether a system is serving care appears in the difficult conversation or costly action it has made more possible.

Private systems are especially vulnerable because their owner writes the categories, chooses what enters them, and decides when the work is complete. No outside person need notice when a warning has been placed in a harmless column. A concern may be marked "later" because later seems prudent, then revisited only after the circumstances have changed. A task may be called “in progress” for months because that label makes abandonment look premature. The language remains polite. The underlying choice has merely been delayed. A useful practice is to give a recurring item a date on which it must become something more definite: done, abandoned, or deliberately renewed with a reason.

There is no virtue in forcing an instant answer where a subject needs time. A rushed decision can be as evasive as endless research when it closes the question before the relevant facts have arrived. The point is to distinguish necessary inquiry from inquiry that protects you from a conclusion already taking shape. That distinction can be made with a modest test. Ask what fact is still awaited, where it might come from, and what action follows if it never arrives. If no answer comes, more sorting may not be preparation. It may be a way of letting the appearance of work stand in for the courage of choosing.

The organiser's danger is not love of order but the hope that enough order will remove the need to lose anything. Deciding does not offer that comfort. It excludes an alternative, spends a limited resource, disappoints a preference, or reveals that the matter cannot be made painless. A system can postpone this discovery by keeping alternatives on the page. A page looks generous, though life does not remain equally open simply because the list does.

That is why the final question has to concern conduct rather than appearance. What will be different by tomorrow because this system exists? If nothing can be named, the work may still have been pleasant and occasionally useful. It has not yet become preparation for a decision. This distinction is not harsh. It gives organisation a purpose beyond its own refinement.

A person who organises well can still be caught by this mistake because the visible signs of care are so close to the visible signs of avoidance, and the difference may remain hidden until a later choice asks whether the system has any authority beyond the comfort it provides. A person may feel productive after refining a plan for the third time, yet the feeling deserves a second look. If revision alters no date or limit, it may not change the action to be taken when the same difficulty returns tomorrow. Good order reduces confusion and preserves what matters. It also makes comparison possible, but it must eventually submit to the question organisation alone cannot answer: given what is now known, what is a person prepared to do?

The question becomes useful when it is asked before the answer is wanted, because that is when a condition can still be stated without quietly tailoring it to protect a preference that has already become dear. No household matter needs to become a formal system, though each needs a point at which preparation ends and a choice begins, since a system without that point can become a graceful method for never learning from its results. When the refinement of a system is more enjoyable than the prospect of acting on it, the pleasure signals a need to ask whether the system is clarifying the matter or merely making delay feel responsible. Visible activity is not evidence of progress unless it leaves a person less free to repeat the conduct that made the activity necessary in the first place.

Deciding is harsher than organising because it gives an alternative a consequence. The person who selects one course leaves another unread, the person who sets a spending limit accepts that some desired things cannot be bought, and the person who sends a reply accepts that the unsent versions will never receive their chance. Such losses are usually small. Their finality is not. A well-made system can keep these losses in view, but it cannot make them disappear. When it pretends to do so, its charm comes from offering permission to delay the moment of exclusion.

This is also why a decision creates a point at which a person can be wrong. A record may later show that the limit was poorly chosen, the estimate mistaken, or the refusal too cautious. That possibility gives a decision its weight. Organisation without a test avoids the same exposure. Its owner can say that more work remained, that the file was still developing, or that the categories needed adjustment. A system earns trust by risking a verdict. It must permit a later fact to show that its rule was sensible, mistaken, followed, or ignored.

The wish to avoid that verdict is understandable. Nobody enjoys discovering that a careful plan failed. Yet the alternative is not safety. It is a condition in which failure cannot be located because the plan never said what success required. The person stays busy, receives the consolations of diligence, and loses the chance to learn which part of the conduct needs to change. A decision may hurt when it excludes. A system that never excludes merely lets the hurt arrive without a name.

One further virtue of a limit is that it makes refusal impersonal at the moment refusal is hardest. A person who has already set a ceiling for the repair need not prove that the contractor is unreasonable, that the work has no value, or that earlier spending was foolish. The next dollar must merely meet a standard established when relief was not being purchased. This may feel less generous than reconsidering every appeal in the moment, yet it is often kinder to the person who must live with the cumulative answer.

The same is true of time: an evening reserved for rest will sometimes be interrupted by a request that sounds worthy, while a rule about such evenings does not claim the request is unimportant but protects an older recognition that a life with no protected time becomes harder to govern. When the rule is changed, the change can be made openly. When it is never stated, every request becomes a fresh contest between the immediate plea and a need with no representative in the room. A system is strongest when it turns an absent interest into a present voice. That role lets the future budget, an unfilled appointment, the need for rest, or an alternative outside the plan speak through a condition written before pressure began. This is not bureaucracy for its own sake. It ensures that the pleasant activity of arranging things does not silence the interests that arranging was supposed to protect.

There is a useful severity in asking a system to say no. The question does not ask whether the system has gathered enough information, displayed it elegantly, or made its owner feel conscientious. It asks whether the arrangement has changed the range of permissible conduct. A calendar that never prevents an appointment is decoration. By contrast, a budget that never prevents spending is an archive. A project board that never requires a choice is a report about indecision. Such tools may be attractive and even accurate. Their accuracy does not make them authoritative.

Authority appears when the owner is tempted to make an exception. The invitation is appealing, the purchase appears sensible, or the further research feels responsible. A working system makes the exception visible as an exception. It forces a person to state why a prior limit no longer applies. That small burden is valuable because it interrupts the easy story that the current case is unlike every earlier case. Sometimes the exception will be justified. The point is that it has met a standard rather than arriving disguised as a harmless adjustment.

This is the difference between a system that serves judgment and one that merely accompanies it. The first carries a prior conclusion into a later moment of pressure. The second keeps the later moment entirely free to explain itself. Freedom of that kind can sound humane. In practice, it often gives the strongest current desire the only vote.

Consider a person considering a substantial change in work, home, or study. Practical material is collected with genuine care: costs, dates, requirements, possible objections, and stories from people who have already made a similar choice. Every file has a reason for being there, and the growing collection can make the matter less frightening by making it seem more knowable, yet none of the pages has to answer the question that will determine the next year: continue as things are, make the change, or decide that change cannot be made now. The collection can expand after any uncomfortable fact because expansion is always defensible. It is hard to accuse someone of being too well prepared. A system that respects judgment introduces a moment when the collection must become an answer, perhaps by setting a date for choosing, identifying the fact still missing, or requiring a comparison between the present course and the best available alternative. Such devices can be revised when a real condition changes, but not merely because the decision has become emotionally expensive. That distinction preserves the proper role of organisation: research remains a way to see clearly, while deciding remains the moment at which a person accepts the cost of seeing clearly. No list can remove that cost. Its honest service is to make the cost visible before delay turns it into a larger one.

The hardest systems to build are those that place a check outside the mood that created them, because a person can promise to spend less while feeling prudent then find reasons to spend when a tempting object appears, or promise to speak more carefully while calm then find the old words waiting when a familiar argument begins. A promise needs a form that survives the change in atmosphere: a limit written down, a day between an impulse and a purchase, a requirement that another estimate be obtained, or a rule that a difficult message is read again before it is sent. Each device is modest, and none can make a person wise, yet each can prevent a passing desire from presenting itself as the whole case. This is not distrust of the self in every circumstance but respect for the fact that a self in one circumstance has access to evidence that a self in another may prefer not to see. The earlier self can anticipate later pressure without claiming to know every future fact, while the later self can revise the rule when facts change without pretending the original limit never existed. Such an arrangement gives memory a practical role, allowing the person who saw clearly yesterday to be heard by the person who wants relief today. Good organisation makes that conversation possible. Bad organisation fills the room with paper until neither voice can be heard.

The real discipline is to let your record become a witness against you when it must. Without that willingness, the record can remain a beautiful account of attention while the underlying habit continues untouched. It becomes more practiced whenever the organiser converts a warning into another object that can be filed or coloured before it is deferred and admired from a safe distance. A system is useful only when it changes what you do next.

## CHAPTER EIGHT

# The Scalper's Clock

Intraday scalping is trading in which a person buys and sells within the same day, sometimes within minutes, seeking small gains repeatedly. Usually, the trader closes the position before the market shuts. A position is stock that the trader has bought, or stock sold short, leaving the trader exposed to a change in price. Closing it ends that exposure. Speed is the point because the desired price movement may last only moments, making delay feel less like caution than failure.

That pressure is not merely background. Judgment happens in an interval, a span in which an initial impression meets a contrary fact, a second thought, or a reason to refrain. Even a brief interval can suffice, but it still has to exist. When an activity compresses it to nothing, the person may keep acting with confidence while the capacity to judge quietly disappears.

An interval is not measured only by the clock. It is measured by what can enter before the act becomes difficult to reverse. Ten quiet seconds may contain a memory of a prior mistake, a glance at a missing fact, or the recognition that the body is trying to escape discomfort. Ten minutes can contain none of these if the person is busy defending the first impression. What matters is not whether a person waited in some ceremonial way. It is whether the first impulse encountered any resistance that had a chance to matter.

That resistance may come from within or from the setting. A colleague may ask a question that exposes an assumption. Written rules may make a preferred action harder. Memory may turn a rush of certainty into a claim that needs proof. Judgment does not require endless reflection. It requires enough room for a contrary fact to arrive before action converts a feeling into a consequence.

That same pattern appears outside markets when a message arrives on a phone while its reader is upset. On reading the first lines, you feel accused and begin typing before the final line has registered, because silence feels like surrender and a reply seems urgently necessary. A sharp phrase is chosen, deleted, restored, then sent while your body is still reacting to what you think it says. A few minutes later, after the screen is dark, the sender sees that the other person was asking for help or trying clumsily to repair something.

Trouble in that exchange is not simply anger. Anger at least announces itself. More deeply, the sender may not notice the absence of judgment at all. A reply has words, reasons, and a target. It may even be grammatically careful, which can make it feel considered after the fact. Yet consideration is not proved by the presence of an explanation. It depends on whether the explanation was available before the message was sent, when it could still have altered the message.

A later apology does not restore the missing interval. It may repair part of the relationship, which matters. It cannot make the original response a judgment rather than a reflex. This distinction can sound severe because ordinary life requires quick replies. No message needs to become an essay. It is that a person needs some practice in recognising the moment when speed has become a substitute for knowing what is being said. Those facts were present, yet the interval in which your first reading could meet the whole message had vanished. An evening may then be spent defending a reply that would never have been sent if the phone had been put down long enough for the first heat to pass.

Silence can feel expensive, while delay can look like weakness, and the feeling is real. It is not always reliable, while a fast reply can have the appearance of decisiveness without the substance. Imagine a meeting in which someone asks for an answer before you are ready, and the room goes quiet while a colleague looks toward you. A person knows enough to say something, though not enough to know whether it is right, and gives a view because an immediate answer seems better than admitting that more time is needed. Those words set the direction, and relief arrives because the silence has ended. Later, walking back to your desk, you remember the relevant email or realise another team will bear the cost. Nothing prevented you from knowing these things, except the pressure that compressed the interval in which they could become active. A pause of five minutes might have changed the answer, though the room made five minutes feel like an extravagance.

A countdown offer works similarly when you are looking at an expensive purchase and a banner says the price expires in eight minutes. You compare a few features, notice the discount, and picture the inconvenience of missing it. That timer becomes the most vivid fact in the transaction. A buyer may not ask whether the item was wanted yesterday, whether its regular price is sensible, or whether another seller offers the same thing without theatre. Even a genuine offer can lead to a poor choice. Urgency proves only that time has been made part of the sale. Modern life compresses intervals everywhere through unfinished messages, waiting rooms, timers, alerts, and the next item in a feed. Such pressure is felt daily even when it has never been named. Naming it matters because an unnamed pressure can disguise itself as the world as it is. Your first task is to notice what urgency has displaced, while often, it has displaced the chance to think. Markets make the pressure unusually explicit because a changing price seems to announce that a chance is forming and vanishing. Information sits beside the button that acts on it, while the result appears at once and becomes material for the next response. There is no walk to another room. There may be no person asking what you mean to do. Its circuit is direct: perception, response, result.

This was the setting in which I traded. I had spent years in work where a preliminary view had to meet material that weakened it. A document could be put down, reopened, then read against a later fact. Those habits did not make anyone wise. They created resistance between first impression and an action that would be difficult to revise, while scalping gave me much less resistance because speed was not incidental to the method. Speed was the method. You can act quickly after preparation, as a driver brakes or a cook catches a falling pan. Such speed may express training already tested in calmer conditions. Scalping asked me to interpret a shifting display while the interpretation itself could expire, rather than execute a settled response to a known emergency. As I became quicker, less time remained for an unfavourable fact to become visible. That is the central loss, while a screen does not announce it.

I had been trained by work that made a first answer provisional. In forty-seven years following my qualification as a lawyer, slow habits had accumulated: read the document again, notice the word that qualifies the confident sentence, distinguish a fact from an assertion, ask what a later reader would need to see. These habits did not guarantee good judgment. They created an interval in which judgment could occur. Here the interval was part of the work, not a hesitation before the work began.

Scalping structurally excluded that interval because the format rewarded the person who treated the changing display as a demand for immediate interpretation, then made a new display available before an earlier interpretation could be examined. The years of training were not refuted by this setting. They were bypassed, which does not show that they had failed. A method that requires a person to decide before slow capacities can enter prevents their use. It prevents their use.

That distinction matters beyond markets. Trained skill can be real while the setting offers no time in which to use it. A careful manager may be placed in a stream of requests that permits no verification. Patient listeners may be drawn into conversations that punish every pause. Competence is not a possession that appears automatically. It has conditions, and time is one of them.

On screen, prices and charts changed, while a chart is simply a visual record of how a price has moved over time. Such a display can reveal a pattern, though a pattern is not a conclusion. Finviz, Trade Ideas, TradingView, and thinkorswim gave me information with speed and clarity. Those tools did what they were designed to do. Their efficiency could not return the seconds I had given away.

Information can improve a judgment only if it reaches a mind before the mind has committed itself to an action. A faster display can make the opposite outcome more likely. It supplies a succession of vivid facts, each one inviting a response before its relation to the previous fact has been understood. More information is then confused with more understanding because the screen remains full. Attention becomes intense while judgment may be absent.

The danger is difficult to see from inside because there is no obvious blank space where judgment should have been. A person sees a price change, recognises a pattern, acts, and sees a result. That sequence feels complete, and its missing part is not visible as a missing part. That is why speed does more than degrade judgment. It can prevent a person from noticing that judgment is not occurring at all.

A quick act gains a story at once. You may say you saw a setup, noticed momentum, or took an opportunity. Those words may describe a perception, though they may also be reasons manufactured after your hand has moved. If explanation comes only after action, it faces a temptation to flatter the actor. This is visible in a message sent in anger, while the story feels coherent because coherence is what stories provide, not because the story governed the act. This is the scalper's clock: it does not merely ask for speed but makes speed look like evidence of understanding. The clock reduces the interval, then treats its disappearance as competence. A person can feel nimble, attentive, and informed while acting too quickly to discover that movement has replaced judgment. Such a substitution is serious.

The consequence accumulates quietly because one action on a screen can seem too small to examine, then a second arrives and a third follows before the day has acquired a shape. Each can be defended as a response to a particular moment, while the day becomes a chain of acts none of which seemed large enough to require a full account. Frequency changes the mind because the tenth response arrives in a person altered by the previous nine. A small loss can create a desire to repair it, while a small gain can create pressure to continue.

Frequency gives this problem an arithmetic: suppose a person loses only twenty dollars on an action that seems too small to deserve an examination. If it happens twelve times in a day, five days a week, for fifty weeks, the arithmetic reaches sixty thousand dollars. The exact amount is less important than the structure. A cost that seems harmless when viewed once does not remain harmless when a format invites it repeatedly. The scale arrives after the opportunities for inspection have passed.

The same calculation applies to time and attention. Six minutes given to a needless response can look trivial. Repeated ten times in a working day, it becomes an hour. Repeated across a year, it can displace work, rest, or a conversation that had no alert attached to it. Frequency hides behind smallness because each event asks to be judged only as itself while the total is built by events excused from judgment.

A life-changing number rarely announces its approach as a single number. It arrives as a series of amounts too modest to interrupt the next one. That is why a person needs a way to count patterns rather than merely experiences. Without one, the format keeps presenting a sequence of isolated moments while quietly constructing a result that none of them, taken alone, seemed capable of producing.

I cannot reconstruct the individual trades that produced my losses, though I can identify the structure in which they occurred. Without a contemporaneous account, memory chooses scenes that flatter it or blurs scenes that do not. This pace made a usable account less likely. A decision that leaves no record is difficult to examine, while the next decision has already crowded it aside.

The small decision is especially hard to examine because the next one appears before the examination has found its language. By the time a person asks why the first action was taken, the second has produced a new reason to attend to it. Review begins to feel like falling behind. That feeling is not neutral, since it turns the absence of review into the price of staying current.

Here lies the sharpest danger of the scalper's clock. Speed does not merely leave less time for judgment. It removes the signs by which a person might recognise that judgment is missing. Movement feels like attentiveness, and an explanation assembled after the click feels like a reason that preceded it. A fresh opportunity makes the unexamined action seem unimportant. The format does not have to persuade its user to reject reflection. It only has to make reflection feel late.

Judgment leaves a trace before it leaves a result. A person who has judged can usually say what was seen, what alternative was rejected, and what fact might later show the choice to have been mistaken. None of this requires a formal memorandum. It requires an interval in which the action has a reason that exists before reward or loss supplies one afterwards. Without that interval, review becomes largely theatrical, because the actor can always explain what happened but cannot show whether the explanation governed the act. This difference matters in every rapid system. A person who buys against a countdown can later describe the purchase, a person who accepts a request in a crowded meeting can later give good reasons for being helpful, and a trader can later point to movement on a chart. Reasons may be accurate after the event while still failing to have been reasons for the event. The record of judgment is not eloquence after the fact. It is the prior condition that could have prevented the action. A fast format weakens that condition by making the next stimulus more interesting than the earlier reason. It keeps the actor busy enough to feel engaged and hurried enough to treat examination as an indulgence. That is how the clock can empty an action of judgment without making the action feel empty.

Once that has happened, confidence can increase as judgment decreases. The person becomes fluent at moving from signal to response. Fluency looks like skill, though it may be skill in obeying a pace that has taken the decision away. A smaller version appears when a day is governed by notifications. An alert interrupts one task, so you glance at it and answer it. A new tab opens, followed by a short search. Another alert appears before you have asked what deserves the hour. None of these movements is dramatic, and each takes less than a minute, yet a person may work continuously without deciding what received full attention. The device has not forced you to abandon your priorities. It has made each interruption feel too minor to require a choice. The cost appears only when you try to say what received your full attention.

A notification system gains power in precisely this manner. Each interruption seems too small to justify a formal decision, so the day is surrendered in pieces. An answer seems courteous, a search seems efficient, and one glance at a price or message seems harmless. By evening, the person has been active for hours without having granted sustained attention to the matter that mattered most. No single interruption appears large enough to indict the system that produced it.

The repair begins with a question that sounds almost too simple: what is this interruption asking to displace? Sometimes the answer will be nothing important. Sometimes it will be the only uninterrupted part of the day. Naming the displacement restores a comparison that the alert was designed to bypass. It gives the interruption a size that its individual duration had concealed.

Review needs a place in the sequence rather than a place after the sequence has become unbearable, since in slower work a person can return to the prior page, ask why a conclusion was reached, and compare it with a fact that later became available. That time is not spare time but the part in which judgment becomes accountable to reality. Rapid activity puts review at a disadvantage because every minute spent looking back appears to surrender the next opportunity, so a person can know review would be useful while experiencing it as a failure to keep up. The format need not argue that reflection is worthless. It makes reflection feel costly at the moment when it would be most valuable.

A workable protection is not a promise to examine every moment with equal solemnity but a boundary between stretches of action and moments of account, where after a set number of choices or a loss or a fixed period no new action occurs until the preceding ones have been named. This returns responsibility to a sequence that otherwise dissolves it. A record need not be elaborate: a few words can establish whether an action had a reason before its outcome supplied one and can later reveal a pattern that memory would prefer to convert into isolated occasions. Without such a record, the mind describes a fast day from inside the story it told while moving through it.

A private rule can protect an interval if it is made before the pressure begins. A person might read a message twice before replying, say in a meeting that a fact needs checking, or close the shopping page until tomorrow. Each rule looks modest, and its purpose is not to make life slow but to keep the first impulse from appointing itself judge. The person who makes the rule is not quite the person facing the screen, though they share a body and a name. The earlier person sees a wider field, while the later one may only want the discomfort of uncertainty to stop. A rule lets the earlier person retain authority when the later one is least willing to listen. Faster access can be useful when it brings material to someone who still has room to consider it. It becomes dangerous when it replaces consideration.

A rule that protects an interval should be specific enough to operate under pressure. “Be more careful” has no force when the message is already open or the price is already moving. “Read the whole message, then wait ten minutes before replying” can be followed or not followed. “Do not accept a deadline in the meeting” can be revised only by naming the reason for the exception. The rule is not a guarantee of wisdom. It is a place where a later action can meet an earlier judgment. The most useful rules are modest because they can survive ordinary life. A person need not become unreachable or treat every purchase as a moral drama. The point is to know which categories of action have repeatedly become expensive when performed at speed. A small delay in those categories can return more judgment than a grand declaration of discipline. The interval is protected by practice, not by admiration for the idea of it.

My intraday scalping turned repeated brief actions into a loss of more than $20,000 over seventeen months. No individual click announced what the total would become. Accumulation did not care that each moment had felt urgent. It counted every moment, while a rapid system can conceal costs by delivering them in portions too small to command attention until the total refuses the story of smallness.

Urgency can be genuine, as when a driver brakes before constructing an argument. A person moves quickly when a child is in immediate danger. In such cases, speed carries a response that was established by prior learning and clear conditions. This danger is different: it appears when the setting declares an ordinary choice urgent because urgency serves the format, a moving price, a filling inbox, a narrowing offer, or a room that cannot tolerate silence.

The distinction is not between fast and slow people. It is between speed that executes a prior judgment and speed that prevents one from taking place. A trained response can be fast because its governing rule existed before the pressure. An impulsive response can be slow in the literal sense yet still lack judgment if it never allows a contrary fact to matter. The clock matters because it decides which form of speed the setting rewards.

The arithmetic of frequency has an ordinary social form as well. A person may answer a difficult message in thirty seconds because silence feels worse, agree to a request in a meeting because the room has turned toward an answer, then make a purchase because a timer has supplied the day with an artificial emergency. Each act is small enough to be explained by its occasion. Taken together, they establish a way of living in which discomfort is repeatedly settled by speed. That way of living can become expensive without producing a dramatic scene. A message changes a relationship, a promise crowds out an earlier commitment, and a purchase consumes money intended for another use. Each result may appear later after the urgent setting has vanished. By then the original decision feels too minor to revisit, and a person is busy explaining the next one. Frequency deserves an explicit count because a daily practice that costs only a little in money, attention, or trust is still a practice. Its cumulative effect belongs to the pattern rather than to the isolated episode. When the pattern is left uncounted, the mind keeps granting each episode the mercy of being small. Totals receive no such mercy.

Not all speed is an enemy of judgment, because a driver who brakes when a child runs into the road acts from perceptions and rules built before the moment, without needing a fresh inquiry into whether a moving car can cause harm. Quick action can be the visible end of slow judgment. Scalping is different because the thing being interpreted changes as interpretation is formed: a price moves, a pattern appears to form, a possible gain seems available, and the meaning of each element depends on what happens next, while the format prizes a response before meaning can be tested and presents the response that outran it as competence. A person can be fully alert in such a setting and still not be judging, because alertness notices change while judgment asks whether change deserves action and what would count against the preferred reading, an operation that can be intense without being reflective, while a fast screen makes the person feel more capable as appraisal is being excluded and willpower remains an incomplete answer when discipline depends on review that the pace will not permit. This is a mismatch between a slow faculty and an environment organised to reward its absence.

Even a fast exchange can prevent judgment when nobody intends to create pressure. A parent hears a child say something alarming at the door, while the clock is already late and a hundred small tasks seem to require an instant response. An immediate reprimand can end the moment, though it may also settle the meaning of a remark before the parent has learned what happened. The temptation in such scenes is familiar: a quick answer restores order. Still, the restoration may come at the cost of hearing what the other person was trying to say. A breath, a request for one more sentence, or a promise to return to the matter later can keep the interval alive.

Work often rewards the same compression by treating availability as a measure of commitment. A request arrives late in the day, and a person can feel obliged to answer before knowing what it will require. A deadline may be accepted, a number offered, or a result promised because a slower answer seems less generous. Later you discover that the promise displaced something already promised. Nobody compelled the answer. The request made speed feel like the only professional response. Protecting an interval may mean writing that you will confirm tomorrow, even when part of you would rather purchase relief with an immediate yes.

An interval is not empty time. It is where comparison occurs. Comparison places the fear of missing an opportunity beside the cost of taking it, the desire to end a silence beside the value of accuracy, or the pleasure of a discount beside the use a purchase will have after its deadline is forgotten. These comparisons rarely take long, but they require that no timer, crowd, or moving display be allowed to decide which side counts. A person may still choose quickly after such a pause. The speed is different because it follows a judgment rather than replacing one.

Repeated urgency can also alter your sense of what is normal. When every message receives an immediate reply, a delayed reply begins to feel rude even when delay would make the reply better. Under offers that demand a decision now, waiting begins to feel like a form of loss. In meetings that require instant certainty, uncertainty starts to look like incompetence. This drift can be resisted by treating a small delay as information. Notice what the delay reveals about your fear, your assumptions, and the people who benefit when you cannot take time. That observation is the beginning of a choice that belongs to you.

Modern systems often borrow the scalper's clock without using a market: a workplace measures responsiveness by how quickly messages receive an answer, a retailer places a timer beside a price, and a social platform rewards the first reply with more attention than the considered reply sent later. Each system gives speed a local reward while moving the wider cost somewhere less visible. No one facing such pressure needs to become slow in every respect, but attention is needed where speed changes the character of a decision. A reply to an unfinished message, an answer given because silence feels worse, or a purchase made against a countdown asks whether urgency has been allowed to choose the reason as well as the act.

That question becomes useful when asked in advance, before a meeting begins, before a sale page is opened, or before an argument invites its old reply. Preparation does not make life controllable, but it makes it harder for a setting to turn an unexamined impulse into a permanent consequence. The interval is a practical possession, the small piece of time in which a person retains the right to change a first answer before it becomes a record, a cost, or a wound. When it is repeatedly taken away, more than money can be lost. The habit of noticing what has not yet been thought can be lost as well.

A market screen is not required to meet this risk. It appears whenever a reply, answer, purchase, or next task is made urgent before its proper weight has been decided. Look for the missing interval, then protect it before pressure arrives. Reading a message to its end before replying, or writing down the reason for a purchase before a timer supplies the reason, can make the interval visible.

In a meeting, a sentence that asks for time can protect more judgment than a polished answer supplied too quickly. It gives a missing fact the chance to arrive before the room commits itself to a story. Pauses do not guarantee a good result, nor do they remove the ordinary need to act under incomplete information. They preserve the condition in which an error can become visible before it becomes expensive.

A person who waits briefly may still be wrong, yet the wrongness has passed through a mind with an opportunity to meet its own resistance rather than merely inherit the urgency of the setting. Speed can serve judgment only when a prior judgment has decided what may be done quickly and what must first be allowed to become clear. No alert, timer, or moving display can make that distinction for you. The interval belongs to the person who refuses to let pressure select both the action and the reason for it.

A pause is not a performance of calm. It is a refusal to let a manufactured deadline decide what evidence may enter a judgment. When the answer truly cannot wait, a person can still distinguish what is known from what is inferred, then leave the unchecked part unsaid. That small division may take less time than the explanation required after an impulsive reply, a careless purchase, or a decision made merely to release a room from silence.

Repeated use turns the interval into a habit. Its value is clearest when it interrupts a response that once would have felt automatic. Urgency need not be removed from life. It must not become the only fact that reaches the person who is about to act.

Before treating an immediate response as proof of decisiveness, name the alternative being refused, the evidence that may be missing, and the consequence that will remain after urgency has subsided. A decision that cannot survive that small description may have been little more than an impulse given a respectable title. The pause may change nothing, which is useful because it shows the action has survived a question rather than outrun one. The interval is neither caution for its own sake nor a theatrical display of seriousness. It is the ordinary space in which a mind can compare its preferred move with the possibility that it has misunderstood the situation or made present relief more important than a later result. It can be built into routine by leaving a purchase in a basket overnight, reading a message twice, or carrying a difficult question out of the meeting in which it first arose. No method can promise that reflection will remove every error. A life without intervals leaves error no place to introduce itself before action becomes consequence. Keep enough time between the impulse and the act for a contrary fact to speak.

CHAPTER NINE

# The Position You Will Not Close

A position can be losing long before it is closed. On screen, the loss may be called the loss unrealised, which sounds provisional and therefore kind. In fact, the word is neither provisional nor kind. It is a number describing what the holding would bring if sold now, and the word unrealised says only that I have not performed the act that makes the number impossible to ignore. That distinction held more power over me than it deserved. I could see the red figure, see the entry price and the current price, and know what separated them. An open position retained a small legal fiction of its own: because I still owned it, because the market might change, because no final instruction had gone out, I could behave as if the loss remained a matter for argument. It was not an argument with the market. It was an argument I conducted privately with myself.

A position is simply something you have bought and still own. Suppose you buy it for $100, then find that it could be sold for $70, an unrealised loss of $30: the value has already fallen, even though you have not sold. 'Unrealised' does not mean imaginary, pending, or safely outside your account. It means that you still possess the thing whose current value is lower. You may keep it. Its price may rise tomorrow. Yet at this moment you have $70 worth of it, not $100. Selling does not reach back and take the missing $30. That market movement did that, and selling changes the form of the loss from an open possibility on a screen into an agreed fact in the record. That is why the order can feel so charged. You are not choosing whether the loss exists. You are choosing whether to stop asking the future to reverse it before you acknowledge it. Once you see that separation, you can consider the future without making it responsible for repairing the past, which is the modest freedom a closed position gives you even when you decide, for reasons that survive a fresh look, to continue holding it.

Nothing has been saved by the delay. Only the admission has been delayed. At that point, a fresh question may still lead you to hold, but it should be a question about the value of what remains, the evidence you have now, and the risk you are choosing to carry, rather than an appeal from your earlier self to be spared the ordinary consequence of having been mistaken. Closing a losing position does not manufacture the loss. By the time the order is entered, the account has already suffered it at the price available in that moment. Holding can change what happens next, of course, a price can rise or fall, or remain obstinately where it is. Refusing to name the loss does not rescue it at that moment. Refusal changes the language, not the arithmetic. I want to be careful here, because a position is not automatically wrong merely because it is below its entry price. Markets move, sometimes sharply, and an honest decision can meet an adverse movement without becoming foolish. A person may have reasons to hold, reasons set before the price moved and reasons capable of surviving a fresh look afterward. That possibility deserves to remain open. It is also not the experience described by the hand that hovers over a closing order then withdraws because the act of closing feels unbearable.

The feeling is familiar even when the figures are modest, but a sale says that the earlier purchase did not work. It says that the opinion expressed by the purchase has met a fact that will not be negotiated away. Before the sale, another outcome remains imaginable. After it, the account contains cash and a record that cannot be dressed in the grammar of possibility.

That is why the click feels larger than it is: it does not take the money, but records that it has gone. It does not turn a sound position into an unsound one, it ends the private extension granted to a position that has already failed its owner. Nothing on the screen is altered except the form in which the truth appears. Still, the hand experiences the act as a kind of self-accusation.

I have known that sensation with intraday trading, although I cannot honestly furnish the reader with a reconstructed example, and that trading produced a serious loss whose particulars I do not remember. That absence is not a small incidental defect. I cannot tell you which position I closed on a given morning, which one I held, or what thought accompanied the delay. My missing record removes an easy defence. If I had preserved a neat sequence of entries and exits, with screenshots and explanations, I might be tempted to make a brief from it. I could arrange the material facts, omit the embarrassing clutter, and give every decision the posture of a considered act. Instead there is the total and the period, the equipment on the desk, and a memory of repeated sessions. Those blank spaces have their own candour.

What I can say is smaller and more certain: at the moment of an open loss, there are always two matters before the holder. One is the economic question: is there now a sound reason to continue holding? Harder to state is the other to state without embarrassment: can I bear to make this loss part of my own record? Those questions can coincide, but they need not.

When they separate, the second can secretly govern the first. A person begins with a price movement then constructs an account of future possibility around the need not to close. An account of the future may use language that sounds analytical. It may mention patience, a reversal, a level, a further look at the information. A useful test is plain enough: would that explanation have been persuasive if the position had been bought by somebody else this minute?

Usually, I suspect, the answer arrives too quickly because a holder does not want a new decision. He wants ratification of the old one. Those are different tasks, though they can occupy the same chair and use the same vocabulary. One looks at what is available now, the second treats the past decision as an asset that needs protection.

A purchase creates more than a holding. It also creates an author who wants protection. Once I have acted, the position carries my handwriting, even when nobody else can see it. If I sell at a loss, I am not only changing the account, I am reading that handwriting aloud to myself. The market is indifferent to this ceremony, which makes it more humiliating that the ceremony can determine what I do.

There is a simple counterargument. It deserves its full weight. If every decline prompted an exit, nobody could hold anything through ordinary movement, and a rule of immediate surrender would be no wiser than blind persistence. Price alone cannot fairly decide the whole matter. A person needs a reason for the original position and a reason for its continuation, and neither reason can be supplied merely by discomfort.

That concession does not save the position held solely because sale would hurt. Instead, it clarifies the question before the holder. Here the issue is not whether a loss may recover, plainly it may. Instead, the issue is whether recovery has become the only argument because acknowledgment has become too expensive. Once that happens, hope changes office: it stops being a view about the future and becomes an anaesthetic for the present.

There is no shame in wanting the price to return. I wanted the price, quite plainly, to return. Wanting is not analysis, though it can imitate analysis with surprising ease. More precisely, it can recruit analysis after desire has already made the decision. My mind is very competent at supplying a reason to wait when waiting postpones an admission. That competence is an important part of the trouble.

Here, "unrealised" helps because it places the pain at a distance. It makes the loss resemble an unfinished document that may be revised before filing. No document is unfinished in the relevant sense when its contents already determine what it would say. Its value has changed whether or not I approve the page. I may refuse to sign it, I do not thereby change the figure.

In practice, an open loss supplies a series of small postponements. I can watch one more movement, wait through one more interval, look once again at the screen, or defer the order until something feels clearer. Each small postponement is defensible when viewed in isolation. Taken together, they form a way of not deciding, and the not deciding is not neutral because the position remains exposed while I preserve the right not to admit what I see.

That exposure matters, but it is not the deepest point. A holder who will not close has put the present under the authority of a past self. Earlier, another self made a purchase under conditions that no longer exist exactly as they did. Now the later self possesses new information, including the fact of the loss. The later self may serve chiefly as counsel for the earlier one.

In legal practice, a previous view had no entitlement to survive its contrary authority. If a fact emerged that altered the position, you did not answer it by saying that you had worked hard on the earlier view. You considered its materiality, meaning whether it could affect the result, and altered the advice if the record required it. Effort explained why a mistaken position was understandable. It did not convert it into a sound one.

That professional habit did not appear reliably at a trading screen. On the screen, every movement felt personal and immediate, while the short intervals invited a different arrangement of the mind. A position could be defended without words. I did not need to write a memorandum or explain it to another person, I only needed to decline the order for another minute. Silence can be a very efficient form of advocacy.

There is an especially ugly economy in that silence. A spoken defence can be questioned, a written defence can be reread, and a reason given to another person can sound thin in the air. A position held in private needs none of those tests. It can persist in the tiny space between noticing and acting, where discomfort says enough to keep the order unentered and nobody asks what exactly has been decided.

At first, the apparent choice is between closing and holding. Beneath it, the real choice is often between accepting a fact and arranging life so that the fact remains formally unaccepted. This is why the open loss can feel less painful despite being economically identical at the moment. It permits a person to retain a version of himself who has not yet been wrong. It lets the account carry the burden while the self remains temporarily intact.

That temporary sense of intactness comes at a price. It makes the loss harder to examine because examination threatens the arrangement that has kept the self clear of it. A new decision becomes harder because it might expose how little support the old one has. Even a small act of correction can then feel like a verdict on character. Meanwhile, the position grows psychologically larger precisely because it has been left open.

Nor need the admission be grand or theatrical. Sometimes it is only the recognition that a reason has expired. I had a reason to buy, I no longer have a reason to hold. That sentence contains no confession of stupidity and no claim of moral superiority. It is an ordinary adjustment to changed information, which ought to be one of the least dramatic things a person can do.

Ordinary adjustments are difficult when the adjustment has a price attached. A change of mind that costs nothing is praised as flexibility. A change of mind that costs money acquires a harder name, even when the money has already vanished from the relevant comparison. We treat the closed loss as the injury and the open loss as its absence. No account shares that preference.

I do not mean that accounts are wise. They are simple, and simplicity can be cruel. An account shows a current value without concern for intention, research and effort, or good faith. That plainness is the account's limited virtue. It does not grant a credit for the effort spent protecting my opinion. It does not increase the value of a position because I find the result difficult to accept.

For that reason, an account can sometimes tell the truth more plainly than its owner. It does not tell the whole truth, it cannot say why a position was taken or what alternative existed. It does refuse one particular lie: a refusal to act has kept the original decision alive. An open position may remain economically exposed. The question it posed may already be answered.

There is another necessary concession before proceeding. People sometimes need time before they act, and a demand for instant admission can be bullying in its own right. A person can be surprised, frightened, or simply not ready to understand what has happened. No decent rule would turn every hesitation into dishonesty. Difficulty begins when time is used not to understand the fact but to avoid its becoming a fact one must own.

That boundary is inward, which makes it easy to evade. No one watching the screen can tell whether I am gathering myself for a measured decision or arranging a delay that will spare me a sentence I do not want to say. I may not know the answer immediately either. Its distinction appears in the quality of the next act: does it test the position afresh, or does it merely protect the old purchase from scrutiny?

A genuinely fresh examination has a particular sound. It does not begin by asking what I paid. It begins with what is true now, what was assumed then, and what has changed in between. I have used three clauses there. I distrust the neatness of them, life does not often submit to such a tidy inquiry. Still, the point survives the phrasing: the entry price has no authority over the next decision except through the feelings it provokes.

That last fact is obvious and strangely hard to live by. A market does not know my entry price. A new buyer and I face the same available price, but only I carry the private demand to get back to where I began. Such a demand looks like a financial objective. In reality it is a demand for erasure.

Erasure is impossible, which is why it keeps a person busy. An earlier act can be revised in the sense that its effects can be limited, but it cannot be made not to have occurred. That closing act says as much without explanation. It brings the past into the account, where the past already is, and stops asking the future to repair a sentence already written.

A recovery, when it comes, can make this mechanism harder to see. If the price returns, the position is sold without the visible loss, and relief arrives with the force of acquittal. Nothing may have been learned except that waiting sometimes works. Or rather, something more dangerous may have been learned: that the refusal to examine a position was the reason the loss disappeared.

That lesson is false even if the money returns. Any return may have followed from the original reasons, from a movement nobody could predict, or from chance, I do not pretend to know in every instance. What it did not prove is that postponing the admission was sound. A fortunate result can give a bad habit an official seal.

In my own trading, the absence of exact records prevents me from grading individual decisions after the fact. I cannot reconstruct which held position recovered or which one deepened the loss. That limit leaves no room for a theatrical claim of perfect hindsight. It does leave the larger record and the uncomfortable probability that I gave too many small delays the dignity of a method.

The smallest form of the problem is therefore not prediction. It is a question of who has custody. When I hold a losing position because I cannot bear to close it, I have handed the next decision to the part of me most invested in defending the last one. That custodian has a conflict of interest. He is not asking what belongs in the account now, he is asking what will spare his predecessor.

In law, a conflict of interest matters because a person may sincerely believe he is acting well while his own stake bends the advice. Sincerity alone is not a cure for it. It can make the danger less visible, since the person hears no internal alarm and mistakes the absence of alarm for independence. The holder of an open loss faces a private version of that difficulty.

He has access to every favourable possibility. He can remember the reason for entry with warmth, locate information that permits continued hope, and feel the fact of the loss as evidence that patience is needed. The contrary evidence has an unfair disadvantage: accepting it requires an action that hurts. No impartial tribunal is coming to equalise the presentation.

The decisive thought may be almost embarrassingly small. I do not know what happens next. That is not a discovery. It does not command a sale. It only removes the pretence that certainty about recovery is carrying the position. Once certainty leaves, the remaining reason must stand on its own feet.

I sometimes confuse confidence with permission to wait. Confidence speaks in a tone that makes delay sound principled, particularly when I have spent time looking at a screen and feel entitled to a return for the attention. Time spent looking does not buy a better future. It buys only time spent looking, and sometimes it buys a more elaborate explanation for why a loss cannot yet be allowed to count.

This was the appeal of the apparatus around my trading. Finviz and Trade Ideas stood alongside TradingView and thinkorswim, making the work look equipped and deliberate. The tools did not cause the loss by themselves. I do not blame them for it. What they supplied was a setting in which another look at the screen could always feel like a responsible postponement.

What the tools could not provide was assent. They could show movement, filter information, and fill the screen with signs that action was informed. They could not perform the private act of saying that the current facts had defeated the reason I had given myself.

Better instruments can increase the temptation to postpone that act, because they make another look seem like work rather than avoidance.

A position remains especially dangerous when it has become a project. Projects conventionally receive an ample supply of patience. Projects are allowed setbacks, reassessment, extra time, and the benefit of a story about eventual completion. A loss needs none of these courtesies. Once I make the holding into a project, I can confuse my devotion to the project with evidence that it deserves to survive.

No one likes to be told that an attachment is merely an attachment. The word sounds dismissive. It can be used cruelly against commitments that deserve care. I do not mean to use it that way. I mean only that attachment alters the burden of proof: it makes a person demand more evidence for leaving than he demanded for entering.

That quiet reversal is the mechanism at work. Entry often requires a reason, however thin, exit comes to require a reason so strong that it carries not only the present facts but the emotional cost of admitting the earlier reason failed. That required standard quietly rises beyond recognition. A position that would never be opened now can remain open because it was opened then.

Seen plainly, that arrangement is not patience at all. Patience waits for a reasoned outcome while remaining willing to hear the reasons against it. What I am describing waits for relief from the need to decide. The outer behaviour can look the same for a time. The difference lies in whether the holder is still available to the evidence.

I have no clean account of the moment when that availability went missing in particular trades. The work of writing this forces me to say that without decoration. I remember the screens, the repeated sessions, and the sense that every new movement invited one more response. I do not remember enough to assign a scene to each dollar lost, which is itself a record of what repetition can conceal.

The loss becomes realised when the order is filled, but the acknowledgment can occur earlier or later. It can occur earlier when a person sees the position clearly and holds for a reason that survives the seeing. It can occur later when the account has recorded the sale but the mind still calls it bad luck, an exception, or a theft. Closing is an act with a distinct consequence. Conceding is the part that gives the act its meaning.

A person can close and refuse to concede. He can sell in anger, blame a temporary movement, and open the same kind of position again with the same untested logic. The screen will show a completed transaction, but nothing in him has changed hands. That matters because the book's concern is not obedience to a mechanical rule. It is the cost of treating acknowledgment as the enemy.

Still, the open position offers the clearest picture of the cost because it holds the entire problem in a single instant. By then the price has already moved against him. The holder knows the fact without needing advice. The unentered order waits in plain view. On one side lies an uncertain future. On the other lies a present fact that feels like a verdict, although it is only information. The resistance arises not from complexity but from the wish to remain unmarked.

Suppose you have pursued a qualification for years and have reached the point where it no longer serves the work you want to do. You may have paid fees, surrendered evenings, passed examinations, and arranged your life around the prospect of finishing. Each new term can then feel like evidence that the earlier terms must be justified. When doubt arrives, you do not merely weigh the next year against its likely value. You also feel the pull of the years already spent. Leaving may look like declaring all that effort wasted. So you continue, perhaps with less interest and less conviction, because stopping would give the past a name you cannot bear to give it. The past cost is real. It may have taught you something. It cannot supply a present reason to continue if the qualification no longer belongs in the life you are trying to build.

You are allowed to keep the learning without paying again for the decision. A small business can hold the same kind of open position. Suppose you have kept it alive through a bad season by putting personal credit behind its bills. At first that support may be a measured bridge: there is a credible order coming, a short disruption, a reason to expect that the business can meet its obligations. Later, the bridge becomes a habit. You transfer another payment because the earlier transfers are already there. You tell yourself that closing would make every sacrifice final, while one more month leaves room for a reversal. The money already advanced becomes an argument for advancing more. A person can become less willing to examine the business precisely because examination might require the admission that the earlier support will not return. The ledger does not make that admission for you. It only shows that personal exposure is growing while the question is postponed.

Your past effort may deserve respect. It does not get a vote on the next payment. There are positions outside the screen that do not display their current value in red. They can remain open for years because nobody supplies a price at the edge of each minute. Their owners can call the delay reflection, loyalty, prudence, or merely the way things are. I will not attempt to name those positions here. You have probably supplied a name for one already.

What makes those positions difficult is not that the evidence against them is hidden. Often it has been available for a long time, waiting in plain sight while the owner gives more attention to the inconvenience of admission than to the reason for it. A closing act might be one conversation, one sentence, one decision not to continue. It may exact a cost greater than money alone. That does not make the cost imaginary.

The screen at least has the decency to show a button. It offers a moment in which the holder can see that the loss and the admission are separate events, even when they arrive close together. I did not always use that moment well. The distinction remains, quiet and exact, beside the order waiting to be entered.

The awkwardness lies in the fact that no external rule can settle the matter in advance. A person can invent a mechanical instruction to sell whenever a price crosses some line, yet the instruction will merely move the same struggle to the moment when it becomes inconvenient, because a rule that has not been accepted in the difficult moment is only a sentence written for easier weather. What matters is the willingness to let present evidence alter the act that follows from it. That willingness matters even when the alteration records a loss the holder would prefer to keep conditional.

For years I worked with files that forced a sequence onto a dispute: identify the claim, identify the facts, identify the authority that made the claim weaker, then advise on what could honestly be maintained. The sequence was not magic, and people could misuse it, but it put a little distance between a desired result and the words used to seek it. At a screen, by contrast, desire and action can sit next to one another so closely that the wish to preserve face arrives disguised as a reason to preserve the position. The proximity is part of the danger, because there is little time in which the holder can hear himself substitute one for the other.

A closed loss is not a moral category. It does not establish that the buyer was vain, reckless, inattentive, or any of the other accusations that flood in once a number becomes final. It establishes only that the price at sale differed from the price at purchase. The larger inquiry concerns what the buyer knew and whether later information was allowed to change the decision. The temptation to convert a financial result into a character judgment may be precisely what makes the mechanical correction so hard to perform. Someone who waits for perfect confidence before closing will wait for a condition that no honest appraisal can provide. Confidence about the past has a peculiar seduction because it promises to turn an uncertain future into a settled explanation, yet the future does not owe the holder an explanatory ending and the past does not become less real because its meaning remains partly unsettled. I can admit that a position has ceased to justify itself without claiming omniscience about tomorrow. The admission is narrower, more modest, and more useful than the grand verdict the frightened mind imagines it requires.

The account is blunt, but its bluntness can create a moment of freedom. It shows what the holding is worth now without offering consolation for the price paid or credit for the effort spent in arriving there. Faced with that figure, the holder can ask whether he would buy this same position at this same price for the same reasons if his earlier purchase had never occurred. If the answer is no, the earlier purchase is no longer evidence in favour of carrying it forward. It is evidence only of the attachment that makes a fresh answer difficult.

There is no virtue in making a ritual of loss. I resist the appetite for severity that can attach to such language. Some people sell too quickly, some hold too long, and a decision made in haste can be as much a refusal of thought as a decision postponed without end. The holder who cannot even put the question of closing before himself has already lost more than money. He has lost the ability to distinguish a reason for continuing from a reason for avoiding an admission that continuation is no longer justified.

When I say that the money is already gone, I mean the comparison that matters at that instant, not an assertion that all future outcomes are fixed. The position may recover after I sell, as it may decline after I hold, and no sentence in this book can make either possibility disappear. What the statement removes is a false privilege claimed by the past: the privilege of treating the entry price as a debt the future is obliged to repay because I find the alternative hard to accept. The market recognises no such obligation, however persuasive it may sound in private.

A person can feel the difference by imagining that the position belongs to a stranger. The stranger has no memory of the entry, no embarrassment to avoid, and no story to defend. He sees only the information available now and the price at which he may act. I do not suppose anyone becomes that stranger simply by imagining him, but the exercise exposes the hidden party to the decision, the earlier self whose reputation has become more important than the question presently before the account. Once exposed, that party can no longer claim to be a neutral observer.

I am writing only three months after the losses stopped. I do not claim the serene distance that would make these reflections easy to deliver. The screens are not an old story to me, nor are the missing records a lesson I can set down with a flourish and leave behind. What I have is the small mechanism, visible each time an order waits unanswered: money can be lost before it is realised while the admission remains suspended in the hand that will not yet close the position. That suspended admission is where the real expense begins. I have to correct one final temptation in my own language: to call every delayed close cowardice would be both satisfying and false, though that puts it too strongly even as a warning. What I mean is more exact: a position becomes dangerous when I protect myself from the acknowledgment already required by the facts, because then the account is carrying a loss while I am using the open position to preserve a version of myself who has not yet had to agree. In that narrow space between a visible number and an entered order, the cost of not conceding takes its smallest, clearest form. It is not a catastrophe or a theory, but a hand delaying the simple act that would let the record tell the truth.

There is a physical quality to the last moment that language about losses can make too abstract. The screen is lit. The price continues to alter by small increments, while the cursor remains poised as the mind supplies another reason not to close. None of those motions changes the fact that the current price has already made its offer. Declining it is a decision with a cost. For a long time I mistook the room left by an unentered order for room left in the facts. Now I see the open position as a narrow space in which a person can either let the record become true or continue, for one more minute, to ask the future to excuse him. When present evidence ends the reason for continuing, let that evidence, rather than the cost of admitting the past, govern the next act.

CHAPTER TEN

# Right and Still Wrong

A result arrives with a force that a reason rarely has. It can be counted, displayed, remembered, and discussed without much interpretation. A win looks like evidence of intelligence, while a loss looks like evidence of failure even when the result says far less than either verdict requires. Even so, that temptation has a practical appeal. Results are public enough to settle arguments. Nobody needs to inspect the tangled sequence of assumptions that produced them, the number appears to do the work. If the account has increased, the decision is called good. If it has decreased, the decision is called bad. Such a rule is fast, comforting but frequently wrong.

A good decision can plainly still lose money. It can be made from the information available, with a sensible estimate of uncertainty and a reasonable limit on what is risked, then meet a fact nobody could know. A bad decision can win by the same indifference of events. Over a short horizon, the result does not cleanse the decision of chance, it increases chance's share in what is seen. This is not a plea to spare people from consequences, which still matter, sometimes very greatly. They are often the reason a decision deserves attention in the first place, and a person who refuses to look at results can shelter almost any folly behind good intentions. A result is an exhibit, not a judgment. It needs to be read against the process that produced it.

By process I do not mean an impressive routine. A checklist can be theatre, and a carefully arranged desk can conceal an undisciplined choice. I mean the actual path from what was known to what was done: the information considered, the assumptions made, the alternatives rejected, and the limits accepted. That path can be examined after the result, although it cannot be reconstructed honestly if no one recorded it at the time. There is the first difficulty for me. I cannot reconstruct the individual trades that produced the loss. I remember the repeated sessions and the equipment, but not the sequence of decisions with enough accuracy to distinguish a careful choice that failed from a careless choice that happened to fail. My lack of a record means I cannot turn the record into a fair trial of every entry and exit. It also means I cannot use the total as a simple declaration that every decision was equally bad.

That restraint matters because result-judging has a respectable disguise, which its defenders call realism. It says that the only thing that counts is what happened, and that any attention paid to reasoning is an excuse manufactured by the unsuccessful. There is a portion of truth in that rebuke. People do use explanation to avoid responsibility, particularly when they want credit for a good intention and immunity from its effects. Realism does not require us to confuse outcome with quality. A surgeon may follow sound procedure and lose a patient to a complication, an engineer may calculate competently and meet a condition outside the design assumptions. I mention those examples only as structures, not as a claim that the work is identical. In each, the result matters terribly, but it cannot alone tell us whether the person's conduct was sound.

A trade follows the same pattern, though the stakes and duties differ. I may take a position for reasons that are available before the purchase, define what would disconfirm those reasons, and still lose because the market moves otherwise. If I then call the decision bad solely because it lost, I teach myself to abandon procedures that may protect me over time. That loss becomes an instructor with no knowledge of the lesson.

Conversely, I may buy because I am bored, hold because I dislike the thought of closing, and later sell at a profit when the price happens to rise. Meanwhile, the account credits the profit with no notation about the boredom or the refusal. If I call that result a good decision, I reward the very conduct that could destroy me on another day. Luck thereby receives the apparent authority of method.

This is the deeper and more lasting danger. Outcome-judging is not merely an inaccurate report about the past, it changes what a person does next. A win tells the winner that the preceding acts deserve repetition, even if those acts had no rational connection to the result. Because the win feels like proof, the false lesson is learned with confidence. In the winner's mind, the lesson does not merely make an error, it installs one.

Suppose you are late for work and drive far too fast through familiar streets. You know the route, the crossings where people step out, and the likelihood that you will arrive safely because most such journeys end without a collision. On this morning the lights favour you, the road is clear. You arrive early enough to make coffee. The safe arrival is real, but it does not make the speeding a sound way to travel. If you treat the outcome as the lesson, you may tell yourself that you judged the gaps well or that the risk was smaller than cautious people claim. You have learned something false, then learned it with the confidence that only a favourable result can supply. A near miss would have taught fear, while a lucky arrival teaches permission. That next journey begins with a bad rule already installed.

The result feels pleasant. Nothing broke. No skill was proved. The method remains poor.

A loss can corrupt in the opposite direction by making a person discard a sound rule because the rule did not prevent pain on a single occasion. A person who has acted carefully may decide that care is useless, or worse, that impulsiveness would have produced a better outcome. That conclusion can feel hard-headed because it is backed by a number. It is nevertheless an inference drawn from too little evidence.

At this point, the phrase "trust the process" is often offered. I dislike it. It sounds like something printed on a poster in an office where nobody has to identify what the process is, who designed it, or whether it is working. It can be used to protect incompetence from scrutiny. A process does not deserve trust merely because it has a name.

A process earns confidence only by being available for criticism before the result is known. It has to state what would count against it. It must be concrete enough that another person, or the later self, can see whether it was followed. Finally, it has to allow for uncertainty without converting uncertainty into an excuse for any outcome. Otherwise it is not a process but a story told afterward.

That distinction is easy to state and difficult to keep. Before a decision, uncertainty makes modest language necessary. After a favourable result, the same uncertainty becomes intolerable because it deprives the winner of a clear claim to competence. He wants the result to say that he saw what others missed. A fortunate event becomes evidence of sight.

I recognise that particular appetite in myself. On the screen, a profitable trade can make a decision feel cleaner than it was. On the screen, the price moves in the desired direction, the position closes, and every hesitation before entry is rewritten as prudence. A loss performs the same rewriting in reverse. In neither case does the result show the decision as it was when no one knew what would happen.

None of this is solved by refusing ever to feel satisfaction or disappointment. Those responses are human and sometimes useful. Satisfaction can mark an aim achieved, disappointment can cause a person to inspect what he missed. I want to be careful here: emotional response is not the enemy of judgment. Trouble begins when the feeling becomes the evidence and the result becomes the only witness allowed to speak.

To inspect a decision honestly, one must return to its original conditions. I need to identify what I knew at the time, separate assumptions from facts, and name the aim I was trying to achieve. This work is not decorative, though it can become so if recited without candour. It locates the decision in the time when it had to be made rather than in the later world where the answer is available.

That later world is a treacherous court. Once the result is known, the path toward it appears inevitable. A person can look back at a losing choice and imagine that the warning signs were obvious, while looking back at a fortunate choice and imagine that his confidence was justified. Hindsight makes a tidy record from circumstances that were not tidy at all. It gives the verdict before it hears the evidence.

In legal practice, I learned that a verdict and conduct are not the same thing. A case can be lost because facts turn out badly, because a witness is believed or disbelieved, because a tribunal makes a choice no advocate controls, or because the governing rule permits no better result. None of that makes careless representation acceptable. It does mean that an honest assessment has to examine the work done, not merely the word printed at the end.

Lawyers understand this for a plain reason. If the verdict alone were the measure, a lawyer would be driven toward behaviours that improve appearances after the fact rather than conduct that serves the client before it. He might avoid hard cases, overpromise in easy ones, or treat every unfavourable result as proof that someone failed. Evaluating conduct is not a sentimental concession. It is the only way to tell whether the professional standard has been met under conditions of uncertainty.

That principle does not make law an exception to life. It exposes a condition that is present in ordinary decisions as well: people act before the world reveals which possibility will occur. We judge the act from the later result because the later result is visible. We neglect the earlier reasoning because it requires effort to recover and because it may leave us without the clean praise or blame we thought we wanted.

A sound review begins by separating two questions that habit fuses. First comes the question of whether the result was favourable. Another is whether the decision was well made. They can receive the same answer, but there is no rule requiring it. A person who keeps them separate has not excused himself from results. He has made it possible to learn from them.

Learning requires a correct connection between act and consequence. If I win by chance and attribute the win to my method, I will repeat an act whose apparent success tells me nothing reliable. If I lose despite sound reasoning and attribute the loss to the reasoning, I will remove a protection because it failed to promise what no protection can promise. In either direction, noise enters the instruction.

The word noise can sound technical, so I should say what I mean. Noise is whatever affects the result without being part of the reasoning I am trying to evaluate. A movement in price that no available fact supported, an event outside the assumed range, or another person's choice that could not have been known can all supply noise. This point is not that such things are unreal. It is that they cannot fairly certify or condemn the judgment made before they arrived.

Some people will hear this as a way of making evaluation too complicated. They may be right to harbour that worry. An elaborate review can become another device for avoiding a simple fact, particularly when someone has lost repeatedly and wants every failure to become a special case. Process itself can be romanticised and protected. It can acquire the immunity once reserved for good intentions.

So the review has to retain a burden. The person explaining a decision must show what he relied on and why that reliance was reasonable at the time. He cannot announce that he had a process and ask to be believed. The process has failed its own examination if its reason was vague or no limit was set. It has also failed if contrary facts were ignored or the explanation appeared only after the result.

For that reason, written records matter considerably. A prediction written before an outcome can be wrong without becoming dishonest. It can be reviewed without the later result quietly rewriting it. An unwritten prediction is easily altered in memory. I know this from the opposite side of the desk: a professional record can preserve the reasons a later story would quietly revise, while my trading record cannot reconstruct the decisions that produced the loss.

For me, the contrast is not remotely flattering. A file can preserve the path of a decision, including the doubts and adverse material that a later narrative would prefer to omit. My trading record, as far as I can now honestly describe it, does not permit that discipline. What I have is the result itself. I have only fragments of the setting. The reasoning that would let me distinguish error from bad fortune is largely absent.

Such an absence creates a temptation of its own. I could use the loss total as a club and strike every decision with it. The resulting story would be satisfying in its severity: a careful man lost money, therefore he had been foolish throughout. It would also be a poor piece of reasoning, because it uses the conclusion to establish every premise. Self-condemnation can be as lazy as self-excuse.

Consider a house purchase in which you want the house badly, the market is busy, and an inspection feels like one more obstacle between you and an answer you have already chosen. You skip it, and the house turns out to be sound. No pipe bursts, no hidden defect demands a large bill, and the purchase settles into an ordinary home. You may feel that you saw through the cautions of other buyers. You may even tell yourself that instinct saved time and money. The fortunate condition of that particular house did not inspect the next one for you or make your omission a method. If you repeat it, you carry forward a practice whose success depended on a fact you did not know. The winning decision is worse than the losing one in this respect: it gives you confidence in the very step that deserved examination.

Good fortune can make care look unnecessary. Luck remembers nothing. A person who wins by luck has a different problem, perhaps the more dangerous one because failure at least produces discomfort that can prompt inspection. Success quiets the urge to inspect and rewards the act before anyone asks whether the act deserved reward. The winner becomes a student of a lesson that was never taught.

Confidence makes that mistaken student exceptionally diligent. He repeats the action, tells himself why it worked, and begins to see the earlier uncertainty as weakness rather than accuracy. Each further favourable result, if one comes, hardens the account. Each later loss can then be treated as an unfair interruption rather than evidence that the original rule had no sound basis.

Admitting luck has a harshness: a desired outcome did not necessarily belong to one's skill, and an undesired outcome did not necessarily expose one's incapacity. People prefer a moral universe in which results distribute credit exactly. It offers a cleaner, simpler story that events decline to inhabit. Skill is not invisible. Over enough decisions, a method begins to leave traces. A person who gathers relevant information, confronts what counts against his view, sets limits before pressure rises, and records the reason for acting will tend to make different errors from a person who improvises under excitement. But "over enough decisions" is doing important work in that sentence. One isolated result is almost never enough evidence.

Nor can a person solve the problem by waiting for some magic number of results. A sound review remains qualitative as well as numerical. It asks whether the decision answered its own question, rested on facts rather than wishes, and confronted the possibility that would make it wrong. The questions are plain, but their plainness does not make them easy.

A good process contains the possibility of embarrassment. It states, before the outcome, what would prove the reasoning inadequate. It permits the later self to say, without drama, that a premise failed or a limit was ignored. A process that cannot produce a clean admission has been designed for self-protection. It may still look quite thorough on paper. Yet it will not teach its owner much.

This returns me to the losing position. A person who has made the continuation of a trade depend on the desire not to realise a loss is not reviewing a process. He is allowing the result already visible to dictate the next act, while pretending that the next act arises from a reasoned view. He turns the wish to avoid a bad outcome into the standard by which the decision is judged. The circle of reasoning then closes around him.

A favourable close can build the same circle. If the position recovers, he may say that holding was correct because it produced a profit. He will have learned nothing about whether the reason for holding was sound at the time he held. More precisely, he may learn a false rule with an intensity that a mere lecture could never supply: never concede a loss, because patience is always rewarded.

That rule is attractive precisely because it contains a fragment of truth. On some occasions, patience is genuinely rewarded. Sometimes a well-considered position goes against a person before it goes in his favour. A refusal to admit this would turn process into a rigid machine, and human affairs do not permit one. The turn comes when the possibility of recovery is used to excuse a decision that had ceased to have any other support.

I can plainly see why outcome-judging persists. The habit makes accountability seem deceptively easy. A manager wants a result, an institution wants a result, and a family wants a result, nobody is comforted by a careful account of uncertainty when the result is painful. The explanation can sound evasive even when it is true. A person who insists on process must therefore accept that he may not receive the praise he wants for good work or the forgiveness he wants for a bad result.

That sacrifice is a real and serious cost. It is easier to worship outcomes because they let us settle the question quickly and move on. Process keeps the case open long enough to establish what was actually done. It asks for candour before comfort. It withholds the satisfactions of quick moral sorting. I cannot claim always to prefer it.

The legal analogy is useful because it is disciplined by responsibility. A lawyer cannot simply say that he followed a process and avoid examination. Conduct is tested against duties, preparation, candour, and the actual interests entrusted to him. At the same time, the fact that a case was lost does not, by itself, prove deficient conduct. The distinction protects clients as much as lawyers.

It protects clients because a profession that punished every loss as incompetence would teach its members to avoid difficult causes and hide uncertainty. Such a system would reward the appearance of success rather than faithful work. It would also make the professional more concerned with being seen to win than with doing what the situation requires. Such an arrangement is corruption, not accountability.

The same corruption appears in a private decision when the outcome alone becomes the teacher. The person begins choosing what will look successful if fortune cooperates, rather than what can be defended before fortune has spoken. He may take risks that are invisible in a win and catastrophic in a loss. He may stop recording his reasons because the result has made reasons seem unnecessary.

My screens did not protect me from that temptation. Finviz and Trade Ideas, with TradingView and thinkorswim beside them, could furnish information and visual order. Their effect was to make the later answer louder, nothing more. They could not judge whether I had acted on a reason I would recognise as sound before I knew the outcome.

The equipment may even have made outcome-judging easier. A screen gives the result a permanent and changing presence, while the earlier reasoning has to be recalled from memory. There, the price is always present. The assumptions are somewhere behind it, perhaps unwritten, perhaps already altered by the movement I am watching. Under those conditions, the outcome has home advantage.

A written record can redress some of that advantage. The record need not be remotely elaborate. It need only state the reason for the act, what would count against it, and what action will follow if that contrary condition appears. I can hear the old professional habit in that sentence. I do not apologise for it. A record is not a guarantee of wisdom, it is a way of preventing the later result from rewriting the earlier mind without leaving fingerprints.

There is a limit to what records can do. They can preserve a bad process just as faithfully as a good one, and a person can write nonsense with great care. No form substitutes for honest engagement with the facts. But without some account made before the result, review depends on memory, and memory is unusually obliging when it has a reputation to protect.

The right question after a result is not whether I feel vindicated or ashamed. Those feelings can be noted, then set aside while I establish whether the decision met its own terms. I need to ask whether I acted for the reason I claimed and ignored what would have weakened the case. I also need to know whether I defined a limit, then abandoned it when it became inconvenient. An answer may condemn the process even after a profit, which is exactly why the inquiry is worth making.

When you review something that worked, do not begin by asking whether you are pleased. Begin with the choice that produced it. Name what you knew, identify what you assumed, and notice which protection the result made seem unnecessary. You do not need to punish yourself for being fortunate, but you do need to refuse the confidence that fortune is offering for free.

A loss may also leave the process intact. That does not make the loss painless or unimportant. It means only that pain has not been allowed to impersonate evidence. The person who can make that distinction is not above consequences. He is less likely to be instructed falsely by them.

There is a quiet moral relief in this, though that phrase risks making the work sound easier than it is. Process review does not remove responsibility. It narrows it to the place where a person had agency. I cannot control every event after I act. I can control whether I looked, whether I admitted uncertainty, whether I made room for contrary information, and whether I changed course when the premise failed.

That is enough responsibility for any honest person. It is also more demanding than the worship of outcomes, because it leaves no place to hide after a win. A profit does not excuse a bad reason. Nor does a verdict erase competent conduct. Both a red figure and a green figure can lie when asked to say more than they know.

The screen continues to offer its simple answer. A number rises or falls, and the colour tells me how I am meant to feel before I have examined how I arrived there. The harder work begins after I look away from it. Somewhere behind the changing price is the earlier self, waiting to be judged by what he knew rather than by what I now wish he had known.

The review of a decision must begin before the reviewer knows whether he is pleased with it. He has to recover the alternatives that were actually available, the information that was available with them, and the point at which he chose one course rather than another, rather than placing the later result at the beginning of the story and pretending that it was visible all along. Only then can success be separated from competence, or failure from the sort of error for which a person was genuinely responsible. There is an uncomfortable implication in that separation. A person may deserve criticism after a profitable result, not because profit is unwelcome but because the means of obtaining it cannot safely be repeated, while another may deserve credit after a loss for refusing a temptation that would have looked sensible only if luck had co-operated. This is not an invitation to distribute praise generously. It is a demand to assign responsibility accurately, which is harder and less gratifying than announcing that the number tells the whole story. Before an outcome arrives, a decision has a texture that hindsight removes. It contains incomplete information, competing explanations, and time pressure. It also contains the knowledge that any action will leave something undone. After the outcome, the mind finds a direct road from the earlier moment to the result and treats every deviation from that road as proof of negligence. Good review has to restore the uncertainty without allowing uncertainty to become a universal alibi.

I know the difference in legal work because an unfavourable verdict did not excuse a lawyer from examining his conduct, but neither did it settle the inquiry. Preparation had to be judged as preparation, candour as candour, and advice by reference to the facts available when advice was given. That standard can be exacting because it asks what a person did with the responsibilities he actually possessed rather than awarding merit to whoever happened to receive the desired result. A verdict can be indispensable and still inadequate. It tells the parties what has happened to their dispute and may create consequences that no account of care can erase. It cannot identify by itself whether the advocate looked for adverse authority, prepared the available evidence, or spoke with proper candour when certainty was not warranted. The profession distinguishes conduct from verdicts because leaving them fused would teach a false lesson after every case. The same false lesson can be learned from a gain. When a hurried choice happens to pay, the person who made it does not merely enjoy the money. He acquires a reason, or believes he has acquired one, for trusting the impulse that came before it. I want to be careful here: an impulse can occasionally coincide with a sound insight, but the profitable coincidence does not establish that it did, and treating it as establishment gives chance authority over the person's next decision.

Results are often too loud for this work. They arrive coloured, counted, and charged with relief or regret, while the earlier reasoning is quiet and may already be fading. A person has to make a deliberate effort to hear it without correction from the answer now visible, otherwise the result will not be evidence among other evidence but an instruction issuing from the loudest voice in the room. I found no machine on my desk that could make that effort for me.

The limitation matters most after success. A loss injures the vanity that might otherwise resist examination, but a win can turn vanity into a duty, because the winner begins defending not simply a decision but an identity newly certified by the outcome. Against that pressure, an honest record is less a diary than a witness: it shows the hesitation, the missing fact, and the stated limit before later satisfaction erases their significance. None of this permits indifference to repeated bad results. If a method produces failure again and again, the reviewer has an obligation to ask whether the premises were poor, whether the evidence was misread, or whether the stated method never governed the decision at all. Yet the inquiry has to remain an inquiry rather than a ritual punishment, because a sequence of losses can tempt a person to seek relief in the first apparent alternative, even when that alternative has no better support than frustration.

The discipline is modest, not glamorous. Before acting, write what is believed, what would weaken that belief, and what one will do if the weakening fact appears. Afterward, compare the act with that earlier statement and refuse both the flattering interpretation supplied by a win and the humiliating interpretation supplied by a loss. The number on the screen may still matter greatly, but it has been returned to its proper place: a result to be understood, not a verdict that teaches by itself.

Outcome cannot be dismissed, but it must be put in its place. A profit may test an idea without proving it, and a loss may expose a weakness without proving that every part of the earlier reasoning was defective. More precisely, each result is a new fact that belongs in the next decision, not a retroactive authority entitled to rewrite the decision that occurred before the fact existed. To learn from it, a person has to ask what the result changes in the evidence and what it does not change in the account of how he chose.

That work asks for an unflattering kind of fairness. After a gain, I need to be willing to say that I may have been fortunate, and after a loss, I need to be willing to say that I may have acted reasonably and still met an outcome I could not control. Neither statement relieves me of the duty to examine what I did, but together they prevent the result from becoming a flattering teacher in success or a vindictive one in failure. The discipline begins in a quieter place, before the green or red number has had time to tell its story.

What I need from a result is not permission to congratulate or punish myself before I understand what happened. I need it to disturb the next judgment in the right proportion and require a look at the premises. A moment of fortune or misfortune cannot explain the whole earlier decision. That proportion is hard to find when the number is moving in front of me, because the number offers a certainty that reasoning almost never can. The screen goes on changing, but the earlier reason, if I have written it down, remains where I left it, waiting for a fairer reading.

At the end of a review, I do not need a story in which I was wise or foolish in every respect. I need a record that distinguishes the reason I had before the result from the explanation I was tempted to give after it, because that distinction leaves room for correction without rewarding myself for fortune or punishing myself for an event I did not control. It is not an easy division to maintain. The outcome is still there, bright and insistent, asking to be treated as proof. But an earlier note can hold its ground against that demand. On the desk, the written reason and the changing number occupy different spaces. Judge the next decision by what you could know when you made it, not by the luck that arrived afterward.

## CHAPTER ELEVEN

# The Arithmetic of a Defended Position

A mistake has a price before anyone says a word about it. It begins when a person buys when they ought not to buy, holds when they ought to sell, gives an assurance they cannot support, or declines to act when action was available. That loss may be money or time. It may be trust, an opportunity, or nothing visible until later. Whatever form it takes, the original act has a boundary. It happened at a particular moment, under particular conditions, and its first cost can at least be imagined.

What follows is less tidy: a person notices the mistake, or is told about it, and does not concede it. He explains it or softens it before he relocates responsibility, asks for more time, then finds a reason why the verdict cannot yet be reached. None of those acts is the original mistake. Each one is a fresh act, performed after the fact that needs defending has already occurred. That distinction is the beginning of the arithmetic.

This error may be small, as when a trader enters a position for a poor reason and closes it quickly, losing an amount that is painful but contained. A professional can make an unsound recommendation and correct it before anybody acts on it. A buyer can notice that an earlier calculation was wrong, revise it, and endure the embarrassment of an amended figure. There is no virtue in the error, but its reach remains limited because somebody has stopped it.

Defence changes the unit of account because the question is no longer what the original decision cost. Extra decisions follow as the person decides whether to keep the position, repeat the explanation, or conceal the contrary fact. Will he spend another hour seeking support and reject the person who has found the weakness? Each choice is a fresh payment required by the first error. Accumulation starts to shape the next decision before new facts have been assessed on their own terms, so pressure begins to look like information. That first loss can be finite, whereas the sequence has no natural stopping point. It continues until the person concedes or circumstance removes the choice.

That is not a moral flourish about stubbornness but a description of accumulation. If I buy a position and it turns against me, the market has supplied one fact: my purchase is now worth less than I paid. If I refuse to close it because I expect it to recover, I have added a proposition about the future. Once I speak or act on that proposition, I acquire an interest in preserving it, not merely preserving the position but preserving my claim to have seen it correctly.

At first the interest can seem harmless, and a person is permitted to reconsider because in many settings he ought to. Prices move, facts arrive late, and an early criticism can be mistaken. To concede at the first sign of difficulty would not be sober judgment but a different kind of reflex. This problem begins when the defence no longer responds to evidence and instead arranges the evidence around the defence.

I know how respectable that arrangement can look, because over seventeen months of intraday scalping I lost more than $20,000. On my screens were Finviz, Trade Ideas, TradingView, and thinkorswim. Nothing about that arrangement resembled a man neglecting to take the matter seriously. That equipment did not make the losses. I do not say that to excuse it. Finviz and Trade Ideas provide what they purport to provide, while TradingView and thinkorswim show what they show. I paid for ways to see more of the market. I did see more of it. Seeing more was easily made to serve waiting longer, trying again, or treating the next session as the place where the earlier session would be redeemed.

That last word needs care, because I am not saying that every trade was an attempt to recover a previous loss; I cannot reconstruct the trades with that precision. I kept meticulous case files across years of legal practice and cannot now reconstruct the individual trades from that period. This gap is not flattering, but it is material. A record would tell me what I did on a given morning, while the absence of one leaves me with the pattern and the total.

That pattern is enough for the arithmetic because an intraday scalper works in a setting that turns every moment into a possible correction of the previous moment. A position closes, another opens, a scanner presents a fresh movement, and the account carries forward what has already happened. At the screen, a person can tell himself, accurately, that the new decision concerns a new price. He can also use that accuracy to avoid the less convenient truth that the new decision is being made by the same person, under the pressure of an unadmitted loss.

A defended position therefore has two ledgers, one recording the external consequences: the amount lost, the work delayed, the strained relationship and the opportunity foregone. Its second ledger records the acts required to avoid admitting what those consequences mean. Its second ledger holds explanations and selective searches. It also holds conversations not had, changes in account, and choices made to keep the old account alive. That ledger is usually invisible because it is written in conduct rather than money.

This invisible ledger can exceed the visible one because money lost can be counted even when the figure is unwelcome, whereas the hours spent maintaining a story appear as research, persistence, or fair-minded caution and rarely announce their cost until a friendship has weakened or a necessary conversation can no longer be held plainly. A person may congratulate himself on containing the original error while the defence consumes resources that never reach a statement, especially when silence, delay, a busy calendar, a new source of information, or a rule invented after the result is known can each perform the practical work of postponing the sentence, “I was wrong.” That sentence may never be spoken aloud. A position can be defended entirely in the privacy of one mind, which makes it cheaper to begin and harder to interrupt. Every defence makes a further defence more likely because reasons, once offered, develop claims of their own. Suppose I say I kept a losing position because the price might recover. That claim may be reasonable on the first afternoon. If the price does not recover, I need an account of why the first reason still governs. Perhaps the movement is temporary, the timing was poor, or the data was incomplete. Perhaps yesterday’s rule was never the rule that really controlled my decision. That defence does not stand still and instead recruits supporting propositions.

Those propositions are not neutral additions, because each one carries a burden of maintenance, by which I mean the obligation to keep treating it as true when contrary evidence appears. A person who has said that more information will settle the matter has trouble conceding when more information fails to do so, or rather when it fails to produce the answer he had wanted. He must either admit that the earlier condition was a device for delay or announce another condition. The original position remains in place because the scaffolding around it has become part of what he is protecting.

Law trained me to recognise this movement in argument. An adverse authority is the strongest rule or decision against the position to be advanced, and a lawyer who encounters it cannot simply pretend that it is not there. He reads it, determines whether it governs, and tells the court about it when the rules require disclosure. That professional task is not pleasant, but its terms are clear. An argument survives by meeting its strongest opponent, not by acting as though the opponent has failed to arrive.

Outside that setting, there is no clerk checking the file for the authority I preferred not to read. There is no opposing counsel with an interest in finding it, no judge asking why it was omitted, and no professional obligation that turns omission into a visible event. I can make a case to myself with one side of the record. More precisely, I can call it a provisional view while treating it as settled whenever another person questions it. That is how a temporary explanation becomes a defended position.

One reason this process feels rational is that every new defence often contains a fragment of truth. Prices do recover, and initial accounts of an event are often incomplete. Critics can be motivated by their own needs and still identify a real weakness. A true fragment makes the whole arrangement difficult to assess, because a person can point to it whenever he is asked about the larger claim. A half-truth is especially useful to a defence because it is not required to be wholly false.

It is a mistake to ask whether each fragment can be defended in isolation because almost always some fragment can. The better question is whether all the fragments justify the time, money, attention, and trust now spent preserving the original position. A defence is an economic activity, though it is usually described as a matter of principle. It takes resources from somewhere, and the account from which it draws is the person's life.

I do not mean that every concession is cheap. Some errors carry consequences that cannot be reversed by prompt candour, and some positions are difficult because the available evidence genuinely conflicts. A person may need to keep working when certainty is impossible. Uncertainty is not an endlessly renewable licence to defer acknowledgment. This difference becomes plain when every new difficulty produces another reason why the decision cannot yet be reviewed.

That second mechanism of compounding concerns the price of surrender. On the day of the original mistake, concession requires one admission: I made the mistake. A day later it may require a second admission: I saw enough to suspect it and did nothing. A month later it may require a third, that I told others or myself reasons that now look less like analysis than protection. Delay adds an item to the bill because delay is conduct.

For that reason, many people prefer to name their delay with a word that sounds passive. They say the matter has not resolved itself, or that they are still gathering information, or that it has not seemed like the right time. Sometimes those descriptions are fair, though often they conceal an active choice to leave the position untouched because touching it would force a reckoning. This calendar is not an innocent witness here, since each day can make the eventual admission more expensive.

That extra cost is social as well as internal. Having insisted to another person that I am right, I can experience a later concession as a threat not only to my view but to my standing. If I have acted on the view, the admission may expose people to consequences they had no chance to avoid. If I have criticised someone else for doubting me, I must now account for that criticism too. Denial accumulates a history, and history has witnesses.

This is why a person can defend a minor error with extraordinary energy. Often, the original matter may no longer be the real subject. What is being guarded is the self that spoke too firmly, dismissed a warning, spent money it claimed to be protecting, or required another person to accept its account. Its size tells us little about that threat. A small error can become expensive when it becomes evidence in a case against the defender's preferred picture of himself.

Suppose you are in a family argument that began with a practical matter: who promised to make a call, who arrived late, whose turn it was to arrange a visit. You know the sort of argument. At first you could settle it by checking a message or saying that you had forgotten. Instead, you say that the other person is making too much of it. They answer that you always do this. Soon neither of you is talking about the call or the visit. You are defending the tone you used. They are defending the accusation they made. You remember the positions with perfect clarity and the subject only in fragments. If you concede now, you fear you must also concede that you were unfair yesterday, that you made them feel foolish, and that you kept the matter alive. You then find a new detail, revive an older grievance, and answer the latest charge rather than the first one. Perhaps the original error was a missed call. The defended position has become a claim about who is entitled to stand where in the family. Its cost is no longer contained by the original subject.

Its original subject has gone. The positions remain. In the market, that picture can be both humble and grandiose at once. I did not think of myself as a reckless man taking blind chances. I thought of myself as a man applying tools, watching conditions, and learning a difficult activity through repeated exposure. Those descriptions were not wholly invented, but they allowed a useful substitution: a serious approach to the activity became evidence that the decisions inside it were serious enough to continue.

Those subscriptions made the substitution easier, and paying for Finviz and Trade Ideas supplied a recurring reminder that I was committed to being informed. The monthly charge did not prove that any trade was sound. It did not improve merely because another month passed. Still, a paid instrument has a quiet persuasive force because abandoning the activity can feel like wasting the investment in the instrument. An expense that ought to prompt a review can become one more reason to postpone it.

This is the familiar force of a sunk cost, but the label does not solve the problem. Calling something sunk means that the money already spent cannot be recovered by spending more. A person can understand that sentence perfectly and still experience the prior expense as an argument for continuing. That feeling does not arise from faulty arithmetic alone. It arises from the wish to make the prior self look less mistaken, and that wish does not yield simply because someone names it.

A firm concession interrupts the escalation because it refuses to treat prior expenditure as a claim on future expenditure. Those subscriptions were paid, the time was used, and the trades occurred. None of that becomes better by offering it another morning. When this is stated plainly, it can sound almost childish, but the mind has a talent for making a plain statement unavailable precisely when it is most needed.

That rising cost of admission has another effect: it changes what counts as evidence. Early in a defended position, a contrary fact may seem useful because it helps the person decide. Later, the same fact feels hostile because it threatens to make the growing debt due at once. The fact has not changed, but its price has. What began as information becomes an accusation, and the defender begins to handle it accordingly.

That is the third mechanism: a person who pays more to keep a position begins to lose the ability to see it clearly, not because he has become unintelligent but because clarity has become expensive. It requires him to count the error alongside the reasons, acts, and omissions added to avoid naming it. To see clearly is to calculate the whole bill: the original error, the days of denial, the claims in between, and the choices displaced by all of it. He must then admit that much of the burden now comes from later conduct rather than from the first act. Few people perform that calculation willingly while they still believe a further defence may spare them from it.

That distortion is practical before it is psychological. He looks for records that support the position and postpones records that might end it. His questions already carry answers compatible with his account. He gives more attention to temporary relief than to disconfirming evidence. These are not theatrical deceptions. They are ordinary uses of attention, and attention is a limited resource.

A man who is defending sees a different object from the man who is examining. That examiner asks what would make the position untenable and goes looking for it. By contrast, the defender asks what permits the position to remain open and goes looking for that. Both may read the same material. Their eyes will pause at different lines, and their hands will make different notes.

That distinction has consequences in professional work. A careful person can construct a competent argument from favourable facts and still fail the more demanding task of identifying the fact that destroys it. This failure need not involve a lie. It may consist only of treating the favourable facts as the real subject and the adverse ones as complications. Once that hierarchy has been adopted, the defender can remain sincere while becoming less accurate.

Sincerity is not a cure. People often defend a position most convincingly when they have stopped noticing the work they are doing to protect it. I want to be careful here: deliberate dishonesty exists. It can do enormous harm, but it is not required for compounding to begin. A person can believe every sentence he says and still select the sentences because they defer the admission he cannot bear to make.

On the screens, the speed of intraday trading narrows the opportunity for this sort of inspection. A price moves, a scanner changes, and another possibility appears. There is always a reason to treat the previous choice as unfinished business rather than as evidence about the method that produced it. That next decision arrives before the old one has been described accurately, which is convenient for anyone who would rather not describe it at all.

I cannot identify the exact point at which my own losses crossed from a series of losses into a defended position. My records are not there, and hindsight likes a clean turning point that real life seldom supplies. It may have happened gradually, through sessions that looked separate at the time and connected only later by the number at the bottom. What I can say is that seventeen months gave every temporary explanation time to acquire furniture.

That furniture was not just software. It was routine, vocabulary, expectation, and the feeling that the next period of attention would justify the previous period of attention. It was the ordinary comfort of having something to do when the alternative was to stop and total the result. Activity is not proof of defence, of course. A defended position often protects itself by remaining busy enough that no one asks what the activity is for.

An error defended over time tends to enlarge its territory. In trading, a position can begin as a decision about price and become a decision about whether the trader is competent. A professional opinion can begin as an interpretation and become a measure of whether its author deserves confidence. A plan can begin as a way to solve one problem and become a test of whether the person who proposed it is allowed to revise himself. Once identity enters the account, the numbers become harder to read.

This is not because identity is trivial. Reputation, self-respect, and a person's sense of continuity matter. The difficulty is that they are badly protected by false persistence. Keeping an error alive does not preserve the self that made it, because it ties that self to a growing record of decisions made in its defence. Candour may wound a person's picture of himself on the day it is offered, but denial gives the wound time to infect the surrounding tissue.

There is a concession before the turn that needs to be made plainly. Persistence can be admirable. Many worthwhile things require staying with an uncertain course after the first adverse result, and a person who retreats at every discomfort will never finish difficult work. Persistence earns its name only when the reasons for continuing remain open to revision. When the reasons are protected from revision, persistence has changed into maintenance.

Consider a manager whose early call becomes policy. A new hire is struggling, a project is late, or a supplier is plainly failing. The manager makes a quick decision for reasons that seemed sound at the time. When warning signs arrive, she treats them as a test of the decision rather than information about the situation. She asks the team to wait another month. When that month passes, the policy is repeated in meetings because changing it would expose the first call. People learn which doubts are welcome and which ones carry a cost. A decision that should have been reviewed becomes the manager's way of showing resolve. You may recognise this pattern at work even if you have never held the manager's job. Once a decision becomes identity, the evidence has to overcome more than the decision. It must overcome the story that the decision proves the manager is decisive. Every meeting spent protecting that story is another expense, and every employee who withholds a warning increases the price of the eventual correction.

A policy can be wrong without making its author worthless. Maintenance has its own logic. It rewards the next action that prevents a decisive test, because a decisive test might end the arrangement. It favours ambiguity over a clear standard, private reassurance over an independent view, and postponement over a date on the calendar. Someone inside it does not usually say, "I am avoiding a test." He says he is being prudent or patient, perhaps thorough or realistic. Such words can be honourable in other circumstances, but here they do work they have not earned.

This structure can be stated without psychologising it. Let the original error impose a cost at time zero. If it is admitted then, the eventual cost is that original cost plus whatever immediate correction requires. If it is defended, the cost at every later point includes the original cost, the new consequences of delay, and the resources spent keeping the defence intact. The important addition is not a feeling. It is a set of actions that would not have occurred but for the refusal to concede.

The additions can interact. Delay may make the original error harder to correct, which raises the cost of admission. The higher cost of admission may increase the incentive to find a further defence. That further defence may distort the evidence available to the person, which makes delay more likely. A loop is formed because each element supplies the condition for the next one. Nothing in the loop requires a dramatic decision. It can run on a succession of small permissions.

This is why the arithmetic is worse than a simple series. In a series, each new amount is added to the earlier amount but leaves the rule of addition unchanged. In a defended position, each new act can make the next act more likely and more expensive. The defence changes the conditions under which the next defence is chosen. It is compounding in the literal sense that the prior accumulation alters the rate of later accumulation.

A person need not be vain for this to happen. He need only have something he values that the concession appears to threaten. The valued thing may be competence or loyalty. It may be consistency, income, peace in a household, or the opinion of someone whose approval has weight. The more legitimate the value, the more persuasive the defence can feel. It borrows moral force from what the person is trying to protect.

Nor is the answer to become suspicious of every sustained view. That would make ordinary commitment impossible. The point is narrower and more demanding: any position that has begun to require repeated exemption from a clear test deserves special suspicion. The test can be an account or a date. It may be an outside reader, a number, or a fact that the defender has an incentive not to notice. If the position cannot survive contact with such a thing, the cost of avoiding contact belongs in its ledger.

I have found the legal analogy useful because it strips away some of the romance. An argument is not honoured because its author feels attached to it. It is tested against adverse authority, evidence, and the account that another trained person can give of the same materials. The advocate may work hard for a client's position, but the work is bounded by duties that make certain evasions costly. Outside that setting, a man may call himself his own advocate and quietly become his own unopposed witness.

That is a dangerous pairing. An advocate's job is to find the strongest available case for a position. A witness's job is to tell what happened. When one person performs both jobs for himself, the persuasive account can displace the accurate one without any moment of conscious fraud. He hears his own explanation often enough that it begins to feel like evidence. Repetition gives it a familiarity that the contrary fact does not have.

The easiest time to interrupt a defence is early, when the original error is still the principal fact. At that stage, the admission may sting, but it has not yet been surrounded by accumulated speeches and acts. A prompt concession also preserves information because the person can still remember what he saw, why he acted, and what warning he discounted. Later, the record fills with later explanations, and the original event becomes harder to see through the debris.

That preservation matters more than it first appears. When a person admits a mistake promptly, he can learn from the decision that made it. When he admits it after a long defence, he must first disentangle the decision from all the later reasons given for not revisiting it. The lesson becomes blurred because the original judgment and the later self-protection have fused. What might have been an error becomes a history.

There is no universal measure for the interval. Some decisions deserve hours of reflection, some deserve months, and some need to be reversed before the next hour has passed. The relevant interval is not a slogan about speed. It is the period after a person has enough contrary information to know the position requires review, yet spends resources preventing a conclusion. He extends the timetable, changes the test, or seeks reassurance that permits one more day of apparent inaction.

A defender often mistakes the absence of catastrophe for proof that the position is sound. Nothing terrible happened today, so the position can be kept another day. The inference is seductive because many errors do not announce themselves with a single decisive consequence. They charge rent instead, and the tenant mistakes the monthly bill for evidence that the building still belongs to him.

That is another reason a written account matters. A current explanation has an unfair advantage over the explanation given at the beginning, because memory edits the beginning to make it resemble the current one. If I do not record what I believed and what would have changed my mind, I can later claim that I always had a more modest view. The defence then rewrites the terms on which it is being judged.

The rewrite can be generous to the person doing it. Memory is not a court reporter, and nobody can preserve every thought exactly. Still, a pattern of revised recollection deserves notice when every revision makes the original position look more reasonable. I want to be careful here: an honest correction of memory is possible. It is sometimes necessary. A correction that always reduces responsibility is not merely a correction but evidence about the direction of the defence.

A position is clearest when it is stated before consequences have made one answer expensive. Before the price moves, the trader can say what would invalidate the trade. Before a professional judgment has produced reliance, its author can say what fact would require revision. Once a plan has collected supporters, its sponsor can still say where it may fail. Afterwards, the same statements feel less like useful boundaries and more like admissions waiting to happen.

This is why a defence so often begins by changing language. The person does not say he was wrong but says the position has evolved. He does not say the forecast failed but says conditions changed. Sometimes the language identifies a real distinction, and no serious person wants to abolish distinctions. Words that preserve every conclusion while accepting none of its consequences do not clarify the record. They insulate it.

One can watch this insulation in the way thresholds disappear. A person begins with a clear point at which he says he will act. When that point arrives, he explains why the relevant number, date, or fact was never decisive after all. The adjustment may be defensible once. If it occurs repeatedly, the threshold has ceased to be a guide and become a prop. A condition that never permits a decision is not a condition in the ordinary sense.

The defender pays for this flexibility twice. First, he loses the protection that a clear rule would have offered before he was invested in the result. Then he loses the information that would have come from testing the position against that rule. He has kept the position open, but he has also made it harder to know whether it ever deserved to be open. The seeming freedom from error is purchased with a growing inability to distinguish error from success.

There is a humane reason to resist such an admission. To concede quickly can feel like treating one's past self with contempt, as though a mistake proves that the person who made it was foolish. It does not. People act from limited information, under pressure, and in conditions that later look clearer than they were. A prompt admission is not a verdict on the whole person but a refusal to make the whole person answer for one decision.

The alternative is harsher than it appears. By defending the error as a measure of personal worth, a person gives it more territory inside his life. He asks every later decision to testify for the earlier one. He becomes less free to change his mind because each change is made to feel like a loss of rank. What began as protection of the self ends by placing the self in service of a position.

There is no technique that guarantees an early admission. A person can write rules and evade them, invite criticism and dismiss it, set a deadline and rename the delay. The point of recognising the arithmetic is not to promise immunity from that behaviour. It is to make the later costs legible while there is still time to refuse another payment. A bill seen clearly is not always paid promptly, but it is harder to keep pretending that no bill exists.

The market supplied me with an unusually visible version of that period. It converted decisions into numbers quickly, then invited me to treat the next number as an occasion for another decision. The loss did not arrive as one large verdict. It arrived in repetitions, which made each repetition seem too small to bear the weight of a larger conclusion. By the time I added the total, the interval itself had become part of what the total measured.

The loss is not only a number about entries and exits. It includes the time during which I could have stopped, the software bills that continued to arrive, and the attention given to making the activity appear capable of paying for itself. I do not know how much of the total belongs to any particular decision. I know that the length of time mattered, because a method repeated over a long period has a different cost from the method abandoned after a week.

The same is true where money never appears. A poor decision taken on Monday may have a modest consequence. By Friday people have adjusted around it, information has been withheld, and alternatives have been abandoned. By the next month, the person who made it may no longer be able to describe the original choice without repeating the later explanations as though they were part of it. The passing days have done work.

A fixed mistake can therefore produce an expanding liability. The liability grows not because the past can change, but because the future is repeatedly asked to finance a refusal to describe the past accurately. Each day of defence is a request for another advance from time, money, attention, or trust. The advance may be granted without complaint. It is still an advance.

This gives a different answer to the question people often ask about errors. They ask how serious the original mistake was, as though its initial drama determines the eventual damage. Initial seriousness matters, plainly. A better predictor is often the interval between committing the error and admitting it because that interval measures how long the defender had to turn one bad act into a system for preserving it. It also measures how many later choices were bent around that system and how much of the final loss belongs to the original error.

The man who makes a large error and concedes it quickly may pay dearly, but he stops paying for its defence. The man who makes a small error and protects it for years may pay in instalments so ordinary that he never notices the whole amount until it has altered his life. There is nothing consoling about that comparison. It does, however, identify the point at which a person has some power: not over the mistake already made, but over the next day's contribution to it.

Suppose you hear a new noise in the car and decide to turn up the radio until a convenient week arrives. At first this is ordinary postponement: you have work to finish, the repair may be minor, and every mechanic's visit seems to invite an expense you did not plan. When the sound returns you tell yourself that it has not become worse, which is not the same as knowing it is harmless. When a passenger asks about it you offer the same answer more firmly because the question now seems to criticise your judgment rather than describe the engine. Weeks pass. You choose routes that make the sound less noticeable and postpone a long drive because you do not want the car tested at speed, while the choice not to know begins to organise other choices around it. You may start avoiding the invoice as much as the repair, since paying it would confirm that the earlier decision to wait had a cost. Nothing dramatic need happen for the position to grow: the radio gets louder, the explanation grows smoother, and the available evidence becomes whatever allows one more week without a garage appointment. When you finally take the car in, the bill may be manageable or it may not. Either way, the arithmetic includes more than the part that failed. It includes the trips not taken, the attention spent suppressing the worry, and the small acts by which you taught yourself that relief from looking was a reasonable substitute for learning what was wrong.

You may tell yourself that this comparison is too ordinary to carry a serious lesson, yet its very ordinariness is the point: a defended position seldom announces itself as a grand refusal of reality, because it more often comes dressed as a sensible exception that lets you avoid one uncomfortable appointment, one difficult message, or one number that would force a revision of the account you have been giving yourself. The next time the noise returns, you may be tired, busy, short of money, uncertain whether a garage will be honest, and reluctant to spend a morning on a problem that still permits the car to start. None of those reasons is absurd. Together, though, they can keep you from asking the only question that matters: whether the price of postponement has begun to exceed the price of finding out. Once you notice that shift, the decision changes. You are no longer deciding only whether to book a repair. You are deciding whether a chain of understandable delays has gained a claim on the next week of your life. That claim does not become valid merely because it has been paid before. You can acknowledge the earlier reasons without asking the later decision to defend them. You can let the car be examined while the original choice remains a choice made under the limits that existed then. The distinction sounds small. In practice it separates a temporary inconvenience from a pattern that recruits your schedule, your attention, and your confidence in your own explanations.

A defended position can be priced without pretending that every difficult matter has an easy answer. Start with the original error, or the possibility that it was one. Then count what has been done because conceding felt too expensive. Delayed conversations belong in the count. So do records avoided because they might make the position untenable. A standard changed after the result arrived is relevant. So is a warning treated as disloyal because it asks for reconsideration. The count requires no self-condemnation. It requires a distinction between the cost of the first decision and the costs produced by preserving it. If no clear test can change the position, it is already charging a cost. If a clear test can be named, give it a date and allow someone else to see it. A private promise that never meets a fact is only another room inside the defence.

An honest review need not demand a public confession or an instant reversal, although it does require you to name the evidence that would make continued defence irrational and distinguish that evidence from the discomfort of admitting what it shows, which are very different burdens even when they arrive at the same moment. Bring in someone who has no need to protect your earlier account, give that person the rule you said you would follow, and ask them to compare it with the facts now available. Their purpose is not to humiliate you but to make the whole sequence visible before the sequence becomes the only thing you can no longer see. If you do this before the position has acquired years of explanation, you give yourself a chance to correct the decision while the correction concerns the decision itself rather than the increasingly elaborate person you fear you will appear to be when you admit that the decision should have been reconsidered sooner.

The next payment is still optional, even after the previous payments have become difficult to count and the person who made them has learned to call them patience, research, loyalty, or simply the ordinary cost of staying the course. When the screens are on, an account can make the interval look like a field of new opportunities. Numbers change, alerts arrive, and the next possible action presents itself as independent of the last. After the screens are off, the room has less to say. The monthly charges remain what they were. The missing records remain missing. Deprived of movement, the defended position begins to look like what it cost to keep alive: a structure built from ordinary acts that seemed separate because each came before the total could be seen. When a position demands another defence, count that defence before you pay for it, then decide whether the original position still deserves the part of your life it asks you to spend.

CHAPTER TWELVE

# The Concession

People speak about changing their minds as though they are waiting for the right fact. A fact arrives, the old view yields, and reason receives its due. That account flatters everybody involved, especially the person who held the old view for too long. It is also usually false, because better evidence is often available long before a defended position is abandoned.

Nobody is argued out of a defended position by better evidence. The defender has normally encountered enough evidence to know that his account is under strain. It may not settle every detail, but it makes delay an active choice. He may not have read every page or heard every critic, but ignorance is rarely the central obstacle. That obstacle is that agreement would cost him something now. Until maintaining the position costs more, the evidence is merely a bill he can decline to pay. The bill remains. Nothing is settled. The debt remains.

This is uncomfortable because it removes a pleasant picture of ourselves. We would prefer to think that we give way when truth persuades us, and sometimes we do. A genuinely new fact can alter a conclusion, particularly where the earlier conclusion was tentative. A position that has been defended through repeated contrary facts is being maintained by something other than the quality of the reasons.

This change comes when the arrangement stops paying for itself. A deadline arrives, money runs out, a person whose opinion carries weight asks for an account, or a written prediction becomes impossible to ignore. That person does not become more intelligent at that moment. The circumstances have changed so that the old evasions cost more than the admission they were built to avoid.

That is the useful part of a rather bleak observation. If concession occurs when maintenance becomes too expensive, the practical task is not to hunt indefinitely for a decisive argument. It is to make maintenance expensive sooner, while the position is still small enough to examine. Its aim is not punishment but to make the costs that already exist arrive on the same day as the decision rather than months or years later.

That distinction matters in every practical device that follows. A device is not good because it improves the quality of a person's private thoughts. Private thoughts can be rearranged with surprising speed once a person has become invested. A device is good when it creates a cost for leaving the question unanswered. It gives the defender less room to postpone the moment at which he has to say what he thinks happened.

I have used the word concession rather than change of mind because it names the price. A change of mind can sound clean and neutral, as though a person has simply moved from one chair to another. A concession says that something was held and that holding it mattered. Letting go may involve loss of face, money, time or authority. The word does not make the act noble but makes the transaction visible.

In the market, the most familiar version is a closing decision. A losing position does not become a loss when the trader closes it. It is already worth less than he paid. Closing merely converts a condition into an admission that cannot be softened by the phrase unrealised. That difficulty lies in that admission, which is why a person can look at the same number for a long time without acting. That account contains a fact, but the person has not yet accepted its meaning.

My intraday trading used four applications: Finviz, Trade Ideas, TradingView, and thinkorswim. Tools can give a person more data and still leave him free to delay the judgment that the data makes possible. Equipment has no standing to insist that its user stop. This is not an attack on information, because good information can reveal a problem and a bad record can conceal one. I want to be careful here: people do change their minds because new evidence arrives, and no sensible practice would close its door to that event. That point concerns the defended position, where contrary evidence has already been admitted at the threshold but kept outside the room. More evidence placed beside the door will not change much if nobody has to open it.

A person who wants a different result needs to alter the incentives around his own attention. He needs a form of evidence that cannot simply be read and admired then set aside. He needs a date that converts delay into a failure to act, a record that makes revision measurable, or another person who can ask a question that cannot be dismissed as an inconvenience when the defender has begun to treat every objection as a failure of sympathy. These are not improvements in character but changes in circumstance.

One useful structure is a written prediction, made before action. It states what is expected, the basis for that expectation, the time it is expected to take and the observation that would count against the view. The later self should not be able quietly to substitute a more flattering forecast after the result is known. It should use ordinary language, because a prediction that cannot later be understood by someone else has been written too vaguely to constrain anyone. That point is not literary precision but preventing the later self from pretending that he expected whatever occurred.

Make the first one tonight. Choose a decision that has a visible consequence and use one sheet of paper or one note that can be dated and sent. At the top, write the decision in seven words or fewer: “Continue the kitchen repair" or "Keep paying for the course." Under a heading marked Prediction, write forty to seventy-five words. That is long enough to name a claim and short enough that you cannot hide inside qualifications. Begin with "I expect" and give the result you expect by a stated date. Add one sentence beginning "because" that names the basis for that expectation. Then write "I will reconsider if" and complete the sentence with a fact that another person could recognise. Add a review date and the name of the person who may read the page. Finish with one line headed Cost of continuing. Keep the page plain rather than persuasive. Leave out the history of your good intentions and every possible outcome. A prediction has done its work if a stranger can tell what you expected, what would trouble that expectation and when you promised to look again. If the page cannot do that, shorten it until it can. Put the date in the calendar before you close the note. Send a copy to the contradictor, or leave it where the two of you have agreed to find it. The object is not a permanent diary. It is one clear commitment that the later self will have to meet in its original language.

A prediction needs a date, because without one a forecast can slide from next week to some time later, then to an undefined future in which it has no chance of being tested and can therefore remain an expression of preference rather than a proposition capable of failing. That date is not a claim that all uncertainty will vanish when the clock strikes. It is a commitment to reopen the question on terms set before the result became personally expensive. A calendar can supply a kind of opposition that private reflection rarely manages.

A prediction also needs a disconfirming condition: "I will reconsider if I am wrong" is not a condition but a gesture toward one. Name the fact, number, event, or failure that would require a review. If the relevant subject cannot be reduced to one number, identify the concrete evidence that would count as adverse authority. That condition may prove incomplete, but an incomplete condition written in advance is still harder to evade than an unwritten feeling.

A good written prediction draws a line between uncertainty and permission. It does not say that a person has to abandon a view at the first difficulty. It says what difficulty will force him to stop treating the matter as settled. That pause is valuable because defended positions thrive on continuous motion. A written line interrupts the motion and makes the earlier self available to question the later one.

This earlier self has an advantage that the later self lacks. He is not yet defending the result, has not incurred the visible costs, and has not begun adjusting his language to fit the evidence. He can be wrong about the future, plainly. Yet he can sometimes be more trustworthy about the terms on which the future ought to be judged. His uncertainty is an asset because it leaves room for an answer he will not like.

Written predictions are especially useful where people work with confidence rather than formal forecasts. A manager can record what a proposal is expected to change and when it will be visible. A buyer can record the facts that justify a purchase and the fact that would make the purchase a mistake. For a trader, the record can state the reason for an entry and the condition that invalidates it. That written statement need not be long. It needs to be recoverable.

Recovery is the part most people omit, because a notebook filled with predictions that no one rereads is a private archive, not a constraint. Put the review on the calendar when the prediction is made. At the review, place the original words beside the outcome and write one sentence: confirmed, not confirmed, or still genuinely uncertain. A person who refuses even those plain categories is not protecting complexity but preserving an escape route.

A sentence after review is not an invitation to perform self-accusation. It is an entry in a record of how well a person sees. Some predictions will be wrong for reasons no one could have known, and some will be right for reasons unrelated to the original reasoning. That record does not promise a perfect measure of foresight. It prevents a person from using a successful outcome to erase a poor process, or an unsuccessful outcome to erase a sound one.

A prediction can be written badly on purpose when the defender who suspects that a record will expose him fills a forecast with qualifications so that any outcome can be called consistent. He may make the time period elastic, define the expected result with words that have no edge, or list so many possible conditions that no one can tell which mattered. Those are not minor drafting faults but the defence appearing at the moment the supposed safeguard is designed. For that reason, give the document to someone else when the stakes justify it. Ask whether that person can tell, without help, what was predicted and what would count as disconfirmation. If the answer is no, the statement does not yet impose enough cost on revision. A second reader does not need to agree with the prediction. His job is to make its terms visible before they can be altered.

A second structure is a deadline chosen in advance. A deadline is not a motivational slogan or a decorative date in a diary. It is a point at which continuation requires an affirmative decision, supported by a fresh account of the facts. Until that point, the person may follow the original plan. At that point, he cannot simply let the plan continue by inertia. That difference between review and continuation is larger than it sounds. Inertia is a form of maintenance because it lets the old choice keep acting after the reasons for it have aged. An affirmative renewal forces the defender to ask whether he would make the same choice now, with the information he now has. He may still say yes. But he has to say it in the present tense.

Deadlines work best when they attach to a decision rather than an aspiration. "I will be more open-minded by Friday" does not give anyone a testable act. "On Friday I will either renew this decision in writing or stop it" does. That latter sentence has a consequence, and consequence is what makes maintenance expensive. It narrows the number of ways a person can call postponement a plan. A deadline does not need to be public to be useful, although public deadlines can have force. It needs to be real enough that missing it creates friction. Put it in a calendar that you actually see. Attach a meeting, a review call, a transfer of responsibility, or an action that cannot proceed without the decision. A date written on a loose page and forgotten is merely a promise made to the most forgiving witness available.

There is a concession before the turn. Deadlines can be arbitrary. They may cause a person to decide before the relevant information has matured, and a badly chosen deadline can replace one kind of denial with another. But an arbitrary date can be revised openly before commitment, while a date that vanishes only after the defender dislikes its consequence has revealed why the structure was needed. The problem is not flexibility. What matters is the flexibility reserved for the position already under pressure.

The deadline should therefore state how it can be changed. Where additional information would genuinely be material, say what it is and set the new date before the old one passes. If another person is affected, give that person the same account. If the rule for extension exists only in the defender's head, it will change exactly when change is cheapest. Prewritten terms make opportunism more difficult, not impossible.

A third structure is contradiction by someone with standing. Advice from a sympathetic friend may be helpful, but sympathy is not the same as standing. That person has enough knowledge of the subject to see the weakness, enough independence to name it, and enough place in the arrangement that the defender cannot dismiss the objection as casual opinion, a meddling gesture, or the complaint of someone who has no right to the record, however tempted he may be to call the intrusion unfair simply because its timing now inconveniences the story he has been telling himself. Standing is not rank for its own sake. It is a source of friction between a person and his preferred account.

That person does not need to be hostile. Hostility can make defence easier because the defender can explain the disagreement as resentment or ignorance. A good contradictor is specific and hard to wave away. He reads the original prediction. He asks whether the stated condition has occurred and listens for the point at which language becomes softer than the evidence. His presence changes the cost of maintenance because evasion now has an audience. The choice should avoid a person who always reassures, one who depends on approval, or one who enjoys humiliation more than accuracy. Choose someone who can understand the decision, keep a confidence and say, "That is not what you wrote," without turning the exchange into a trial.

Choose the contradictor before the position becomes important. A person selected after trouble begins will be tempted to select someone who already agrees, or someone too distant from the facts to ask a useful question. Select a person who has permission to be inconvenient. More precisely, give him permission in writing or in a conversation clear enough that neither side later mistakes politeness for the rule.

An agreement can be modest. Once a month the other person may receive the original prediction, the current result and the reason for continuing. It may say that he can ask one question which the defender will answer without changing the subject. It may say that he can call for a pause when the stated disconfirming condition occurs. The prior grant matters more than ceremony. It need only create a moment at which silence stops passing for assent. A contradictor is not there to decide every issue for you. Handing over all responsibility is another way to avoid judgment, because it lets the person say he merely followed someone else. The purpose is narrower. Another person makes it harder to keep changing the terms of the case without anyone noticing. He supplies the adverse authority that private life otherwise lacks.

Some readers will resist this because they do not want to expose an uncertain plan to another person.

The resistance is understandable, because a plan can be private for good reasons and not every part of a life belongs on a table for inspection. Yet privacy and insulation are not the same thing. If a position carries enough consequence that its defence may cost you dearly, the wish to keep it entirely beyond contradiction deserves a closer look.

The fourth structure is a rule made by the version of a person who is not yet committed. This is perhaps the plainest form of self-protection. Before the position exists, that person decides what will happen if the disconfirming event occurs. It is written as an action rather than an aspiration. It may read: "If this happens, I stop." It may read: "If the deadline passes, I review with another person." If a cost is reached, a new written decision is required before continuation. An exception is recorded before the rule is set aside. The purpose is not to eliminate discretion. It is to prevent discretion from becoming a private word for continuation when pressure starts selecting only the facts that promise relief.

Such a rule does not predict the future. It accepts that the future self will be tempted to negotiate with facts that the present self can see more calmly. The rule shifts part of the decision upstream, to a time when the defender has not yet begun to need a particular answer. It is the same reason people set out documents, controls, and instructions before an emergency rather than during one. Pressure alters the value of every excuse.

The language needs to be exact: “I will be sensible” has no operational meaning when a person is frightened, hopeful, or embarrassed. “I will stop when the stated loss occurs” can be checked by looking at a record. “I will revisit the decision if the promised result has not appeared by the stated date” can also be checked. A rule that requires a good mood in order to operate is not a rule but a hope wearing official language. No rule can cover every circumstance, and a rigid rule may produce an absurd result when a genuinely new fact changes the situation. This is the second concession before the turn. Exceptions are sometimes necessary, and a system that pretends otherwise will quickly lose credibility. An exception needs its own written explanation and a new review date, made before the original rule is ignored. An exception without those terms is simply a repeal written under pressure.

The point is to make departure visible, because when a person breaks a private rule silently he can later forget that it was ever a rule. When he records the departure, names the reason, and schedules a review, the departure becomes evidence about the position rather than a hidden alteration of it. The record may show that the exception was wise. It may also show that every exception ran in the direction of continued commitment.

For someone trading actively, the rule can concern a period rather than a single position. Intraday activity moves too quickly for elaborate reflection at each moment, which is part of its danger. A person can decide before the session what amount of loss, what number of failed entries, or what departure from the stated process ends the session. Once the condition occurs, he stops rather than negotiating with the screen. Now the rule applies. The rule does not guarantee a good trade but prevents one bad period from demanding a second audience.

For a person spending money, the rule can require a fresh written justification when a project exceeds its prior limit. The justification needs to say what new information supports further spending, not merely how much has already been spent. That distinction matters because the prior spending will be the loudest fact in the room. It has no claim on the next amount unless a new reason gives it one.

Suppose a person has hired someone to repair a leak. Work begins from a manageable estimate then the floor has to come up. A second estimate arrives. A deposit has already been paid, the room is unusable and the prospect of beginning again with someone else is exhausting. That is the moment at which prior spending starts to impersonate a reason for new spending. Before authorising the next amount, write down the original estimate, the current total and the additional work now proposed. Write what result the new money is supposed to secure. Ask the contractor what would make that result impossible or what further cost is reasonably foreseeable. Set a date for a decision after the answers arrive. Give the page to someone who is not living in the disruption and ask that person to read it before approval of the change. It is not a form for making every repair adversarial. It prevents inconvenience from deciding by itself that any further price is preferable to stopping.

Suppose an open position is an argument with a relative that has continued long past the subject that began it. One person may have become certain that the other must first admit what happened, while the other has become equally certain that the first version leaves out the part that injured them. Each new exchange brings back an old example and gives the argument another small investment of time. A page can be made for this without pretending that a family disagreement is a calculation.

Write the claim being defended in one sentence. Then write what is expected to be different after the next conversation, the date by which that difference should be visible and the conduct that would count against the account of the dispute. A good contradictor for this decision is neither the relative's enemy nor a loyal friend. It may be a person who knows neither party well enough to take sides but can recognise when a promised conversation has become another occasion to restate the charge. Tell that person the condition that will end the effort to win the argument. At the review, ask whether the conversations have produced the change written down or merely produced more material for the case. If the answer is the latter, concession may mean dropping a demand for agreement that has become more important than the relationship or the peace of leaving it alone. That does not prove either person wrong. It records that maintaining the position is now costing more than the result it can reasonably produce. The page cannot decide what either person owes the other. It can stop repetition from being called a plan when repetition is all that remains.

For a person responsible for a plan, the rule can require a review by someone who was not responsible for proposing it. The reviewer does not need to invent a better plan. He needs to compare the plan's original claims with the current record and ask whether the stated conditions for continuation have been met. This is less flattering than a presentation full of current activity. It is more likely to reveal whether activity has become a substitute for result.

The same structure can govern a commitment that appears too private or too ordinary to deserve a record. Suppose a person keeps paying for a course no longer attended because it was once expected to change work. The monthly charge is small enough to ignore. The explanation is ready: attendance may resume when life settles down. Put that explanation on the page. State the number of sessions to be attended before the next billing date and the result expected from them. State what will happen if neither occurs. Choose a review date three days before the charge renews, not three days after. Tell a friend with no interest in encouraging a preferred self-image that the page will be sent on that date. If renewal is sought, write a new reason before renewing. "I have already paid for it" is not a new reason. Continuation may be sound. The page simply requires a distinction between a current purpose and an old hope that has become expensive to abandon.

When the review date arrives and you want to move it, do not move the calendar entry first, because that easy act turns an appointment with the record into a private decision to postpone the record. Open the original page and write the request for more time beneath the prediction, together with the date on which you made the request and the fact that supposedly justifies it. An extension has only two respectable grounds: information named in advance has not yet arrived, or a genuinely new fact has made the old test unfit for the decision. In either case, name the fact, set one new date and send the explanation to the contradictor before the old date expires. If neither ground exists, keep the appointment. Read the prediction aloud if you have to. Decide whether to stop, continue under a fresh written reason, or take the stated exception and record it as an exception. Do not call the extension a neutral act. It is a new decision to maintain the position. It deserves the same account as the first decision.

On the page for the unused course, a finished prediction might say that you expect six sessions within the next six weeks to show whether the course gives you a usable skill in the work you actually do. It might say that you will reconsider if those sessions do not occur or if you cannot name one occasion on which the skill has changed a decision. The cost line should state the charge, certainly, but also the time spent telling yourself that renewal remains a plan. At the review, place a mark beside each stated condition. Then write one of three words: continue, stop or extend. “Continue” requires a reason that did not merely exist when you first enrolled. “Stop” requires no apology. “Extend” requires the new fact, the new date and the contradictor’s copy before the billing date passes. A page written this way is not a form for displaying virtue. It is a small arrangement that makes your future explanation answer to words chosen before you had a reason to soften them.

Start with one decision that has a visible consequence. Do not begin by trying to place every thought under inspection, because that creates so much administration that the system becomes another project to maintain. Pick the recurring decision whose continuation is easiest to excuse. Make one page for it, name one review date, and choose one person whose question you will answer.

On that page, separate facts from forecasts. Facts are what have already happened and can be checked without interpretation. Forecasts are what you think will follow and are necessarily less secure. Defended positions often survive by mixing the two, so that a past fact gives borrowed authority to a future hope. Keeping the categories separate does not solve the decision, but it prevents a person from calling hope a record.

Write the cost of continuing as well as the hoped-for benefit. People usually describe the danger of stopping because that danger is immediate and easy to picture. The cost of continuing is dispersed across time, attention and other opportunities. That makes it easier to omit. A written line about that cost is not pessimism but an attempt to put both sides of the decision in the same room.

When the review date comes, do not ask first whether you still feel attached to the position. Attachment is expected, especially if you have invested effort and announced your confidence. Begin with the original condition and ask whether it occurred. If it did not occur, record the new fact that permits continuation and set the next review before you leave the table. The action turns a vague continuation into a renewed decision with a visible author.

If the condition did occur, pause before searching for exceptions. Do not let the search begin to write the conclusion. An exception may be justified, but a search for one places the defender in the familiar role of counsel for his own preferred result. Let the contradictor speak first, or wait until the next day before writing the exception. A little delay is not cowardice here, because it gives the earlier rule time to be heard before the current preference edits it.

The system will sometimes produce a result you dislike. That is not a defect. A safeguard that never interferes with what you want is a form of decoration, and a decorated defence is still a defence. The useful discomfort is the small cost paid early, before the larger cost has acquired reasons and witnesses and a history of its own.

Over time, the record may reveal a pattern more useful than any single verdict. You may find that your predictions are sound but your time estimates are poor, or that you ignore one kind of contrary fact, or that extensions almost always point in the same direction. Those observations give you something specific to alter. General promises to be wiser rarely survive contact with a defended position, but an observed pattern sometimes does.

Do not wait for confidence before using the structure. Confidence is often what the structure is designed to test, and waiting for doubt to become overwhelming gives the defence a long head start. Use the page and the date while the position still seems ordinary. The best time to arrange a future interruption is before interruption feels necessary.

A person can also state the rule aloud to himself before acting. It is an old-fashioned act, perhaps, but it makes the later negotiation audible. "If this condition occurs, I will stop and review" sounds simple because it is simple. When the condition arrives, the silence that follows will no longer feel like neutrality but like a choice not to honour words already spoken. None of these arrangements guarantees good judgment, because a person can write a clear prediction, hear a fair objection and still decide to continue for reasons that later prove poor. Their value lies elsewhere: they make that continuation an act which has to be described against an earlier account rather than a drift which acquires its explanation after the event. Writing a condition in advance does not remove uncertainty, yet it prevents uncertainty from serving as a general licence to ignore every fact that makes the preferred course less comfortable. Another person cannot supply your judgment, but the right person can make you state whether you are revising a conclusion in light of new evidence or merely preserving the conclusion by changing the test.

Plainness has another advantage when the pressure rises: a brief prediction leaves little room to confuse a change in language with a change in mind, especially if the prediction names both the hoped-for result and the fact that would make continuation harder to defend. A date established before attachment develops gives you an occasion to examine the position when examination still feels optional, rather than waiting until the same examination feels like a threat to money, status, comfort or the story you have already told other people. The contradictor should not be asked whether you are a good person or whether the outcome feels unfair, because those questions invite sympathy and produce little evidence about the decision. He should be asked whether the condition occurred and whether the written explanation now matches the record. If you find yourself embarrassed by that narrow question, keep the embarrassment separate from the answer, since embarrassment may be the early price of concession but it is not a reason to alter a fact that can still be read in your own handwriting.

That is why the structure should be ready before a decision becomes a defended identity, when you can still choose a date without suspecting that the date has been chosen to force surrender, choose a contradictor without testing whether he will take your side, and state a condition without immediately searching for the language that will later make the condition disappear. If you cannot bear to write such a page for a decision that absorbs your money, your hours or your attention, that reluctance is not proof that the decision is wrong, but it is evidence that continuation has already acquired a protection which the evidence itself may not deserve. A safeguard becomes real only when it can require an unwelcome answer at the moment when you most prefer a story about exceptional circumstances, and that requirement must come from a page, a date or a person that existed before the exceptional circumstances became a reason to keep the position open. Once that record is in place, you may still decide that the condition was incomplete or that a new fact justifies a different course, but you have to make that case in the presence of the earlier rule rather than quietly replacing the rule with whatever the current pressure permits.

Keep the evidence with the prediction. A link, a printed page, a note of the source or a saved record can prevent later disputes about what was known at the time. The purpose is not to build a case against yourself. It is to preserve the actual basis for a decision before subsequent events make every earlier fact look either obvious or irrelevant.

The structures work together because each closes a different route of escape, with the written prediction preventing revision of the past and making the first account available for comparison. The deadline prevents endless delay, while the contradictor prevents private reinterpretation. Delay has a price. The precommitted rule prevents the current self from having exclusive power over a question in which he is already interested. None of them makes concession painless. Each makes maintenance less free. They also make a person more careful before commitment. Knowing that a prediction will be read later makes you less likely to write a sentence that has no meaning. If you know that a date will require renewal, you are more likely to distinguish a short trial from an open-ended commitment. If you know that another person can ask about a condition, you are more likely to name a condition that could actually occur. The cost arrives before the error has had time to grow.

A structure fails when it belongs only to the person it is meant to restrain, because the moment that person faces a consequence he dislikes is the moment at which he has the strongest reason to edit, postpone, or quietly abandon its terms. That does not mean every safeguard needs an institution. It means that the safeguard needs some feature that cannot be edited at the instant editing becomes convenient. A timestamp can provide that feature, as can a calendar invitation, a shared document, an automatic transfer, a standing meeting, or an agreement with another person. The form is less important than the resistance it supplies.

It is tempting to set very harsh rules because harshness feels serious. That temptation can be another performance, because a rule so severe that you abandon it at the first inconvenience teaches the wrong lesson: rules are theatrical and cannot be lived with. Set a rule that you can follow when the ordinary pressure comes, then make the act of altering it visible. A modest barrier used consistently is stronger than an impressive barrier ignored twice.

Make the review brief enough that it happens: a prediction can fit on one page. A renewal can require ten minutes and three questions: what did I expect, what happened, and what fact now justifies continuation? That is enough for many decisions. Long reviews invite the defender to bury the answer in material, while short reviews force him to name it.

The questions need not be accusatory: "What did I expect?" returns the person to the record made before he had a stake in the outcome. "What happened?" asks for an account rather than an excuse. "What fact now justifies continuation?" requires a present reason rather than a recital of prior effort. Each question narrows the room in which a defended position can hide. At this point, a person may say that he already knows when he is rationalising. He may be right on some occasions, and self-knowledge is useful as well as better than self-deception. But the relevant moment is not the calm moment after the decision but the moment when continuation feels necessary and surrender feels humiliating. A device exists for that moment, when knowing is least likely to govern action.

I do not write this as someone who can point to a perfect set of records. I cannot reconstruct the individual trades, and that absence leaves a generous amount of room for the mind to arrange its later account around the result it prefers. That limitation is part of the case for a written record, not an exception to it. An account that exists only in memory is most malleable when it matters most.

My four applications did not impose the kind of discipline I needed. They offered information, alerts and charts and further ways to observe movement. None required me to state a prediction before acting, stop after a preselected condition, or answer to a person with standing to challenge the next trade. I had paid for instruments that enlarged the field of possible action. I had not built an instrument that could tell me to leave it.

The difference is not between sophisticated people and unsophisticated ones, because a sophisticated person may be better at defending a position precisely by having more plausible language available to him. He can recognise the adverse fact and explain why it is not yet decisive, devise a further review instead of accepting the result of the first, and turn intelligence into a maintenance department. That is why the structures must be simple enough to survive cleverness: a clear prediction is hard to improve retrospectively without showing the improvement. A date is hard to miss without leaving a mark. A fair contradictor can hear the shift from "this will happen" to "this could still happen." A precommitted rule may be broken, but it leaves a fact that the person must explain.

Concession is not a performance of humility. It is an action taken when the record no longer supports continuation, whether or not anyone is watching. The word can still sting, and sometimes the consequences will be severe. But a prompt concession stops the defence from recruiting another day, another reason, another claim on attention. It returns the person from the theatre of explanation to the ordinary work of deciding what to do next.

The practical test is not whether a system makes you feel more prudent. It is whether it will force a visible choice on the day you most want to defer one. Before a significant commitment, write the prediction and its disconfirming condition. Write the review date and the person entitled to ask about it. Then arrange the calendar or document so that the review occurs without requiring a fresh act of enthusiasm. The uncommitted self has only one advantage: it can still decide what the committed self will find inconvenient before attachment starts calling the inconvenience unfair. That advantage disappears quickly once the position is open and the mind begins to furnish the room around it until the furniture starts to look permanent. A date on a calendar, a page bearing your earlier words, and a person authorised to read them are small things. They are small enough to set in place before the room fills, and solid enough to make a door where there might otherwise have been only a wall.

## CHAPTER THIRTEEN

# The Reexamination

That period ends, and the screens do not suddenly become innocent because I have stopped looking at them. They sit where they sat before, capable of lighting a room and making urgency look like work. I leave them dark more often now, without pretending that their darkness has settled the questions that attended their use. That is an action, but it is not yet an explanation, which would require a record I do not possess and a steadiness I am not prepared to claim.

In the first weeks, an odd emptiness settles because nothing demands that I look for movement or rewards me for declining to look. A habit that filled short spaces in a day leaves those spaces exposed when it is removed. Many decisions can be postponed without injury. I also notice how readily the mind supplies a reason to fill the opening.

I am writing only a few months after the losses stopped, close enough for embarrassment to retain its temperature and too close for much wisdom. This account of seventeen months has not ripened into a neat lesson. It has become more troublesome because the number remains firm while its internal history remains indistinct. More than $20,000 is clear, whereas the individual acts that assembled it are not.

Across my years in the practice of law, I kept files. A file was never merely a storage place for paper, though it had that practical use. It prepared an answer for a later inquiry about what I knew and what I did with it. I do not mean that every file was immaculate. I mean that the obligation to leave a trace shaped the work while the work was happening.

My trades have no comparable trace that I can now use. There were repeated short-term sessions with many chances to act, but I cannot rebuild their order with confidence. Memory offers texture rather than evidence, although I remember being absorbed and feeling a next opportunity arrive before the previous one had been considered. That is not enough to make a reliable history.

This fact is more than a private embarrassment. It deprives me of the kind of story in which a person locates a foolish moment and describes it precisely before leaving it behind under a bright label. I cannot say which screen gave me the wrong impression on a particular day, or which stock became the occasion for a bad decision. Nor can I claim that every decision was bad, because the result alone does not carry that proof. No missing account invites imagination. No ledger returns.

It does, however, alter what I now require of an account I give myself, leaving me less interested in a flattering reconstruction than in the blank places where reconstruction fails. A gap has a habit of being treated as harmless when nobody else can see it, especially when the person who might inspect it has benefited from not doing so. In professional work, a gap tends to attract attention because somebody will eventually need to rely on the record. Alone, I had allowed absence to pass for privacy.

There are two desks in my memory, although they did not stand in the same room or belong to the same years. At one I dealt with matters that arrived in folders and left, when they left properly, with some account of why a course had been taken. After the day's work, I sat at the other desk in front of screens, watching information announce itself and disappear. From the first desk, I learned to ask what I had missed. At the other, the next signal felt more important than the question.

That contrast can be overstated, because law did not make me a model of patience and a screen does not remove a man's capacity to pause. I want to be careful here: the trouble is not that one desk was moral and the other corrupting, since each offered a different arrangement of incentives and attention. One preserved enough time for doubt to take a seat, while the other made doubt look late. When I practised law, no matter began with complete information: incomplete facts and varied recollections could be corrected by documents that changed the confidence with which a person first described his own position. Ordinary discipline meant keeping on without pretending that more looking would guarantee a result. It included adverse authority, the authority that cuts against the position being advanced. One did not become fond of it, but one learned that failure to confront it did not make it disappear.

At the evening desk, no opposing advocate appeared. No one required me to set out the strongest reason for leaving a position alone or for ending a session. I could see contrary movement and call it noise, or read a discouraging result as a temporary complication. Unease could then become another reason to watch.

None of this means that a lawyer is incapable of making a poor decision, or that a person without legal training is incapable of sound one. That would make training either magic or useless. It is neither. Training works within arrangements that call for it and sometimes enforce it. I ceased practising law in 2016, but the habits it formed still shape the language in which I inspect what happened. Their presence does not establish their control.

What I keep returning to is the interval. At the law desk, a conclusion usually had to survive time, including the ordinary delay in which an initial view loses the authority of its first appearance. It survived reading and checking, sometimes followed by the disagreeable arrival of material that should have been found earlier. On the screens, perception pressed directly against action. It was not always literally at the same instant, but close enough that the feeling of recognition could take the place of a reason. That compression matters because judgment needs somewhere to occur.

I had treated speed as a feature of the work. In one narrow sense it was: intraday scalping involves short holding periods, and the activity would be something else if time did not matter. The pressure of a short holding period also altered what I took myself to be doing: I called a reaction a decision because a decision was the respectable word available. Language can grant a pass before thought has caught up.

In the months since, I begin noticing small intervals that used to pass unremarked, not as revelations but as ordinary parts of a day that no longer require an immediate answer. A telephone can ring without being answered at once. An email can remain unanswered while I reread it. A question about a property or a mortgage can wait long enough for me to find out whether its first formulation is sound. These are ordinary acts, not a new discipline I have mastered.

Still, the unused moment has become visible. It is not empty, because it contains the possibility that the first explanation serves the person who produces it and that a second explanation deserves time to arrive. I had known this in professional settings for years. Knowing it at one desk did not make it available at another, which is a fact I would prefer not to need.

A man can pay a surprising amount for a way of avoiding that fact. The paid screens supplied a recurring cost that never had to announce itself as part of the loss. No arithmetic accuses me. It waits.

I do not blame the services. Finviz and Trade Ideas supplied what I paid them to supply, and TradingView and thinkorswim were not concealing a remedy from me. A tool can offer information in a cleaner display or a quicker route to a decision. It cannot decide what the information means. It cannot make a person accept an answer he finds unwelcome. I had not bought a guarantee, although I often behaved as though the equipment made my conduct more defensible.

That is a difficult distinction to keep clean. Paying for information feels different from paying for distraction. Each payment has a receipt and a service name, enabling the user to describe a sensible purpose for it. I can still describe sensible purposes for all four applications. What I cannot say is that their presence gave me a method for stopping when the method was not working.

During the period itself, the monthly charge had an almost virtuous quality. It marked seriousness, or rather it allowed seriousness to be inferred from a visible form of preparation. I did not merely watch a screen. I had arranged access to professional-grade tools and returned to them with intention. That account of myself was not entirely false. It was incomplete in the place that mattered. The receipt remains.

A receipt records an exchange, not whether the exchange made the buyer wiser. This is obvious when stated outside the atmosphere of desire, and nearly invisible within it. Those subscriptions helped me maintain a setting in which there was always another thing to inspect. They did not oblige me to ask whether inspection was becoming a substitute for decision.

I can see now why better information appealed to me so strongly. It resembles the preparation I had trusted in other work. Before offering advice, one gathers the documents and checks for the fact that changes the answer. A person who does less is not being modest about uncertainty but leaving work undone. That comparison had force, which is why it carried me so far.

But the comparison breaks at the point where information becomes an alibi. In a file, more material can narrow an issue or expose why the first account cannot stand. On a screen, more material can also deepen concentration without changing the act that follows it. I had confused intensity of attention with revision of belief. That confusion was useful to me, because it allowed activity to count as reconsideration.

I am not saying that every form of research conceals a refusal to decide. That claim would be both arrogant and foolish. Some decisions improve only when a person delays them long enough to learn what he did not know. Correction does not require despising information. It is to notice when information leaves the proposed action untouched.

This requires a question I do not always want to ask: what fact would change my mind? I do not put it to myself ceremoniously each morning. I sometimes fail to put it at all. But its absence is easier to recognise now, particularly when I feel the old urge to make preparation do the work of a conclusion. A position that cannot name its adverse fact is not strong merely because its holder has spent time on it.

At my current work, I still hold Maryland licences as a realtor and mortgage broker. Those roles make disclosure a practical matter rather than an abstract virtue. A material fact is material because it may alter somebody's decision, and the person handling information does not get to reserve that fact merely because the transaction would be easier without it. Such a rule is not an insult to the professional but an aid against the professional's most convenient blindness.

I have begun to hear that word, material, in a less flattering key. The loss is material, plainly, as is the lack of a usable trade record. This does not prove a particular mistake, but it shows that I lacked a way to inspect the repeated acts while they were still occurring. Once named, these facts do not produce a remedy by themselves. No cure follows.

There is a temptation to make the reexamination into a new performance of competence. I could design a tidy system that labels the evidence and makes the recent past look as though it has already been processed. I am capable of making a tidy packet. The older desk trained that capacity well. A tidy packet, however, can be another way of getting past the part that has not yielded.

What has not yielded is simple to state and hard to inhabit, because it leaves no tidy cause to isolate and no single act on which to place the whole burden. I do not know exactly what I believed during the trades that kept me returning. I know the broad setting: paid screens and brief decisions ending in a loss that grew beyond anything I could call incidental. Beyond that, I have impressions and an account balance of feeling, neither of which I would accept as proof from another person. Candour requires an unsatisfying sentence. I do not know.

That sentence has changed its character for me. In practice, saying that a fact was not known could be the beginning of necessary work. It could also be an evasion, depending on whether anyone then went to find out. Here there are things I cannot find out because the moment has passed and the record was not made. The loss of access is part of the cost, though I do not know how to measure it.

For a while I wanted the missing particulars to relieve me. Without a dependable sequence of trades, surely I could not be held to a conclusion about the whole. That is lawyerly reasoning of a poor sort. Complete proof has its place, but a person can use its absence to avoid the weight of what is plain. The plain facts are sufficient to keep me from returning to the old account of myself.

That old account was not grand. It was made of modest claims: I was learning, I was preparing, I was attending carefully. Each could contain some truth, yet together they made it possible to avoid a larger proposition, namely that the activity was not becoming more intelligible as I continued it. A statement can be accurate and still function as concealment.

It is tempting to call that self-deception and leave the matter there. The name has the advantage of being familiar. It lets the speaker sound severe without having to describe the mechanism. More precisely, I gave favourable facts a place in the foreground and allowed unfavourable facts to remain in the room without controlling the decision. That is less theatrical and more dangerous.

The reexamination has not made me suspicious of every confidence. Without some working confidence, a person cannot give advice or complete ordinary tasks. Constant hesitation is not candour. The issue is whether confidence has a way to receive an adverse fact before it becomes expensive to receive it. I had such ways when somebody else had standing to ask for them.

Alone, I mistook privacy for independence, with no external person or record that would expose the gap. That freedom felt efficient, yet it meant that the only person required to interrupt my version of events was the person who benefited from preserving it. I had placed the reviewer inside the position under review. There is no drama in saying that this was a poor arrangement. It is merely accurate: a person with a personal stake cannot always be impartial, but he can make impartiality less optional by arranging a recorded pause or another person's question. I do not write that as a recipe capable of protecting anyone from every error. I write it because I had treated the absence of those things as neutral.

Since then, I try to make small acts inspectable before they become settled. I write down the reason I am about to prefer one course over another when the reason seems unusually urgent. Sometimes the act itself makes the urgency look thinner. Sometimes it does not, and the writing simply records that I proceeded without enough resistance. The page is not a tribunal, but it is less accommodating than memory.

I also leave decisions overnight when their supposed speed is not real. That sounds elementary because it is elementary. I had spent years knowing why it could matter. The difficulty lies in recognising the occasions on which speed is being claimed rather than required. An interval can be refused long before anyone admits refusing it.

The practice is imperfect from the beginning. I do not make a note every time. I do not always notice when I have begun to argue with a fact rather than consider it. Some days I catch myself composing the case for what I already want before I have described the alternative. On those days, the old fluency is still available. It has not become foreign merely because I have named it.

There is a more ordinary consequence of the loss that I had not anticipated: when I now reach for a quick explanation in any part of my life, I notice the small bodily relief that follows, and the relief tells me less about the explanation's truth than about its convenience. I do not regard every convenient answer as false, because that would merely reverse the old error and make suspicion a new vanity, but I have become wary when an answer arrives with no doubt and an unchecked fact. Such answers have often been prepared by desire before reason arrives. The change is not dramatic enough to display to anyone, which may be fortunate, since display would give me another role to play: the man improved by his losses, the man made prudent by an expensive warning, the man whose hard experience now entitles him to instruct others. I do not trust that role. I can keep a statement open a little longer than I used to, particularly when the statement protects my opinion of myself, and allow the first discomfort to remain without immediately constructing a reply to it. Discomfort is not always right, but its disappearance is not always evidence that it has been answered. This is slower than the screen was, and sometimes tiresome, because silence provides none of the quick satisfactions of a moving display. It offers neither a fresh signal nor the impression that a person has kept pace with events, yet it can make a fact audible before it becomes expensive.

The distinction between an interruption and a cure matters. An interruption may only prevent a person from doing the next foolish thing while leaving the old desire entirely intact. I have no reason to suppose that a few months of restraint rewrite years of habit. What changes first is smaller: I can sometimes see the wish to continue before I have translated it into a principle. Seeing it does not compel me to act well, but it removes one excuse for acting without inspection. Routine entries can look dull beside the pressure of a live question, yet their dullness is part of their protection: they require a matter to be described while its terms are still capable of correction, rather than after a preferred account has absorbed the troublesome detail. I did not give trading that form of resistance. I had information, but I did not keep a contemporaneous account adequate to show what information I treated as decisive or why. The distinction troubles me more now than it did during the trading. Information can arrive in abundance and still leave no record of judgment. A record forces a person to choose words that can later be compared with conduct. There is no way to create that missing record after the fact without pretending. I can write about its absence. I can describe the broad facts that remain, but I cannot supply the missing causes from the mood of recollection. Memory is an interested witness when the person questioning it is also the person who needs an answer.

So I resist the temptation to make this book more complete than the experience permits. Its gaps are not a literary device. They are not a modesty I can wear with satisfaction. They show where I failed to make myself answerable while an answer might have changed something. The absence remains after the screens go dark. There are also days when the reexamination seems self-regarding, when I wonder whether I am placing too much weight on a loss that nobody else is obliged to study. That thought is fair as far as it goes. A person can turn contrition into another occupation and use analysis to avoid ordinary responsibility. But the proper limit on self-absorption is not denial of the material fact. The material fact is now part of the furniture of my days. That fact appears when I consider the cost of a service or hear myself say that more preparation will settle an uncertainty that may not be settled by preparation at all. It has made no philosopher of me. It has made certain sentences harder to say without hearing their second meaning. I used to admire a person who could keep moving under uncertainty. I still do, when movement is required and the uncertainty cannot be removed. What I admire less is movement that calls itself necessary because stopping would expose the reason for moving. The difference can be difficult to see from inside it. Perhaps that is why an interval needs a form more durable than mood.

A written reason is one such form, although it has no special moral standing. It can be selective or simply false. Still, the act of putting a reason into a sentence delays the hand by a small amount and gives the sentence a chance to reveal what it omits. That chance is modest. I have learned to value modest chances. The point is not to make every private act public. Privacy has its proper place. So does the freedom to decide without a committee nearby. I had turned privacy into exemption: exemption from recording an acknowledgement while it could still have practical use. That was more freedom than I knew how to carry. For the moment, I am trying to carry less of it alone. This does not mean that another person takes charge of my decisions, or that I have located a permanent external guard against error. It means only that I am less eager to protect every conclusion from interruption. The difference may prove temporary, but it is nevertheless the difference available now.

That is why I distrust declarations of recovery. Recovery suggests a known condition from which a person returns to a prior sound state. I do not know that such a state existed in the simple form the word implies. I had professional experience and a capacity for care; I also had a way of making an unfavourable conclusion wait. Both are mine, and stopping does not establish that I now understand why I stopped. The losses stop at a fixed point, and that stopping is the boundary of this book's evidence. A boundary can be necessary without being explanatory. I have not discovered a single thought that overpowered every other thought, or any moment in which clarity arrived separate from the accumulated force of the figures. I reached a point at which the numbers would no longer fit inside the account I had been giving myself.

Even that sentence needs correction: the numbers had not changed, whereas my willingness to set them beside the account had changed. For a long period, the loss could be treated as a series of separate outcomes while I went on using the same equipment and returning to the same kind of session. At some point the series became a whole. I cannot locate the exact day. I do not want to pretend that I can.

Conceding the whole does not make the separate events visible. There is no recovered ledger hidden behind the admission. I cannot now identify the trade that ought to have ended the matter, because I cannot identify the trades in a form I trust. The lack of particulars keeps the reexamination from becoming a prosecution with a satisfying exhibit. It leaves me with a conclusion that has less detail than I want and more force than I can evade.

A lawyer is taught to distinguish an inference from a fact. The distinction remains useful here: the fact is that the loss followed intraday scalping of various stocks. My explanation of the causes is necessarily an inference, though it is not a casual one. The inference is that I defended continuation more successfully than I examined it. I do not say this to turn a complex period into a single moral defect. Market losses occur for many reasons, and a person can make a sound decision that loses. But a system that leaves no usable record of its own repeated decisions has forfeited a claim to call itself careful merely because its operator was busy.

That last word, busy, has become suspect. Busyness is not false work. I do not want to mock the ordinary person who has too much to do. Yet it can provide cover for a refusal that would be harder to sustain in silence. A crowded screen and a paid subscription make silence less available. They make it possible to mistake constant response for scrutiny.

The screens are off beside me while I write this, their black surfaces holding none of the menace I assigned to them in the first weeks after I stopped. They are objects. A person can use them badly, then make them carry too much of the blame because blame is easier to place on a thing than on an arrangement of attention. I know that. Still I prefer their darkness.

A dark screen produces an interval of another kind and does not demand a reaction or give immediate evidence that a man has acted promptly, nor can it flatter him with activity. In that absence I hear the small evasions more plainly. It is the sentence that begins with a reason and ends by preserving the same position. The sentence has not lost its power, but it has become audible.

Some readers will find this excessive. The loss is substantial, but it does not confer a special right to turn every decision into a hearing. That objection has force, because a life cannot be conducted by cross-examining each passing inclination. The point is not to put a barrister in charge of breakfast.

Yet a defended position often asks for less ceremony than people fear. It may ask only for a note made before action or a day allowed to pass. Those are small intrusions, yet they become difficult precisely when the position has begun to depend on their absence. I had learned to admire elaborate forms of preparation while leaving the simplest interruption unbuilt.

For a moment, the book belongs with you before it returns to my desk. You have an open position somewhere, even if it involves no market and carries no name that would sound dramatic. You may be defending an argument about work, a purchase, a friendship, a repair or a plan that was once sensible. Your own interval exists as well: the minute before sending the message, approving the charge, taking the next appointment or deciding that no further thought is needed. It may be short. It may be the only place in which the first explanation can be tested before it becomes a commitment. The defended argument will have reasons. Some of them may be good. The point is not to become suspicious of every confidence, but to notice the point at which confidence no longer permits an adverse fact to alter the next act. An interval need not be long enough for you to solve the matter. It need not make you calm, but it must be long enough for the fact you would prefer not to name to enter the account before action seals the account. Your own record can be a date in a calendar or a sentence written before the difficult conversation, yet it should require you to say what you expect and what you will do if that expectation fails.

Nothing in that pause guarantees that you will choose well, but it deprives a defended argument of the claim that it had no opportunity to meet the evidence before it asked you to continue. No act of writing gives you certainty about a course that is genuinely uncertain, nor does it spare you from the embarrassment of changing course after you have spoken with confidence, but it makes a later explanation answerable to the earlier moment when the consequences were not yet asking for protection. To recognise that a position has become defended is not to confess that it is false, because some positions survive serious inspection, but it is to admit that you need a form of inspection which does not vanish simply because the answer has become inconvenient. Your fear of looking may be reasonable when looking will cost money, alter a relationship or require you to retreat from a public claim, but fear does not make the cost less real. It does not make the unexamined decision less of a decision. A written condition has value precisely because it may confront you on a day when the convenient account feels more compassionate, more prudent or more realistic than the plain fact you chose earlier as a reason to stop. No reader needs to turn every uncertainty into an inquest, yet any position that has begun to consume time or money without a clear test of its continuation deserves more than the comfort of being left alone.

Suppose a noise begins in your car and appears only now then. You turn up the radio because the journey is short and the noise does not occur every day. A garage gives you an estimate that is inconvenient, so you decide to wait until the next service. The waiting has a respectable story: you need more information, the car is still running and the expense can be delayed. Each reason may be true. Still, you can give the delay a form. Write down the noise as you hear it, the estimate and the date by which you will obtain a second opinion or authorise the work. Tell someone who uses the car with you what that date is. If the noise changes or the date arrives, do not begin by composing a fresh explanation for waiting. Look at the earlier sentence. You may decide the repair can still wait. You may decide it cannot. Either way, the decision occurs in an interval that was made before the radio became part of the argument.

Your defended argument may be less visible. Perhaps you keep postponing a conversation with a person you care about because the present quiet feels easier than the risk of speaking plainly. You tell yourself that you are waiting for the right occasion. You may be. The claim should still have a date and a condition. Write what must be true before you will speak, what change would show that waiting is helping and what date will make you reconsider the silence itself. Ask a person who is not enlisted on either side to read those words when the date comes. That person is not there to order a conversation or decide who is right. They are there to notice whether your standard for action has moved every time action becomes uncomfortable. You retain the judgment. You also lose the easy claim that nothing has been decided while delay continues to decide for you.

There is a temptation, especially at the end of a book, to convert that observation into assurance. I could say that I now possess the interruption, that the interval is restored, that the two desks have been reconciled. I cannot say those things, because the law desk belongs to a period of my life when work came with identifiable duties to others. The evening desk belongs to a recent period that I still cannot fully narrate.

What connects them now is not a lesson completed but an unease I am trying not to smooth away. At one desk, somebody might ask to see the basis for a conclusion. At the other, nobody did. I am beginning to understand how much of my better conduct depended on the prospect of that question, and how little pride there is in calling that dependence a private strength. It is, at best, a fact about the conditions under which I functioned better.

I do not know what will become of this knowledge. It may harden into a habit, or remain a sentence I can write more readily than I can live. I have seen enough of myself to regard both outcomes as possible. The useful work is not to predict which one will occur. It is to leave the question available before I have an interest in closing it.

The reexamination therefore has no clean last entry. I have not recovered the trades. I have not transformed the loss into an asset by describing it. The subscriptions remain part of the arithmetic: Finviz at $39.50 a month and Trade Ideas at $254 came to $293.50 a month, roughly $4,990 across the period. The figures do not explain which moments mattered most, which is precisely why their firmness is so unsettling: they survive every qualification I can make about haste, uncertainty, or an incomplete record. They show that a series of ordinary decisions may acquire a force that no one of them was ever made to bear. So do the evenings spent in front of professional-grade equipment and the ordinary days on which I could have stepped back but did not. Nothing in the writing refunds either money or time.

What writing does give me is a slower setting in which a sentence cannot vanish with the next signal. I can put down a claim and watch its weakness emerge while it is still on the page. I can revise a word that made me sound more certain than the evidence permits, and the revision remains visible rather than being carried away by a later movement on a screen. This is not redemption, only a form of record.

Record matters because memory is so ready to appoint itself counsel. It knows how to find a decent motive and introduce a qualification just before a conclusion takes hold. I have used all those moves in ordinary life, not only in front of screens. The page lets me see the move after it has been made. That is later than I would like, but earlier than never.

There are moments when I miss the old density of the evenings. I miss the impression that every minute contained a possible improvement, even though I now doubt that it did. The admission is not a recommendation but a recognition that an activity can be costly and still provide something a person is reluctant to surrender. If it offered nothing, stopping would require no reexamination at all.

Perhaps that is why the dark screens are not a final answer. Their silence can become another pose if I use it to congratulate myself for abstaining. A screen turned off is not proof that its owner has learned to see. It is only a screen turned off. I need that plainness.

Near two in the morning, the house is quiet in the way houses are quiet when their inhabitants have run out of useful tasks. I am at a desk in Maryland with the screens dark and a sheet of paper beside the keyboard. On the paper is a sentence I have crossed out twice because both versions tried to settle the matter. I leave the third unfinished, and do not turn the screens on.